Laura Linn

INTO THE FURNACE

Fighting to make it as a movie actor

MEREO
Cirencester

Laura Linn

INTO THE FURNACE

Fighting to make it as a movie actor

Mereo Books

1A The Wool Market Dyer Street Cirencester Gloucestershire GL7 2PR
An imprint of Memoirs Publishing www.mereobooks.com

Into the Furnace: 978-1-86151-849-1

First published in Great Britain in 2018
by Mereo Books, an imprint of Memoirs Publishing

The address for Memoirs Publishing Group Limited can be found at
www.memoirspublishing.com

The Memoirs Publishing Group Ltd Reg. No. 7834348

The Memoirs Publishing Group supports both The Forest Stewardship Council®
(FSC®) and the PEFC® leading international forest-certification organisations. Our
books carrying both the FSC label and the PEFC® and are printed on FSC®-certified
paper. FSC® is the only forest-certification scheme supported by the leading
environmental organisations including Greenpeace. Our paper procurement policy
can be found at www.memoirspublishing.com/environment

Typeset in 12/18pt Century Schoolbook
by Wiltshire Associates Publisher Services Ltd. Printed and bound in Great Britain
by Printondemand-Worldwide, Peterborough PE2 6XD

This book is dedicated to my dear family:

Geraldo Pedro Linn

Balala Campos

Joana Quintana

Mariana, Antonio and Joaquim Abensur,
my lovely nephews and niece

Graça Cristina Campos

Marcelo Campos

And special people in my life

Rovena Zanchet

Cintia Fowlks

Thandi Puren

Maria Teresa Tschiedel

Paula Lavratti

Reine Swart

Georgina Gomes de Figueiredo

Andre Frauenstein

Elbie Frauenstein

And to my grandmother and my late grandfather,
Vininha and Lelio Campos.

Contents

Preface

"Acting is not about being someone different. It's finding the similarity in what is apparently different, then finding myself in there." - Meryl Streep

To be an actor, you must be completely open to everything that surrounds you. You must observe the world, the people, everything, and let every little moment and every detail touch your soul, body and mind. You must breathe into the deep valley of your soul every experience, and at a certain point, you must also let go. The good experiences and the not so good ones. The cheerful moments in your life, the tough moments, the heartbreaking ones too.

To be an actor you must be in tune with your inner self; you must be sensitive, you must know how to listen. This is such an important and essential part of acting: listening. To truly listen to others, not just wait for your turn to speak. Listening means to be present in that moment, right there. And being present means that you are taking it in, every word, and letting each one of them affect you for real. Listening is not merely hearing. Listening is reacting. "Listening is being affected by what you hear. Listening is active." - Michael Shurtleff.

There are so many acting techniques, such great teachers and so many ways to discover yourself as an actor. No right or wrong. And there's never an end; it's an endless learning process. Acting is not an easy math equation, like $1 + 1 = 2$. Acting is truly connecting to your feelings, to others' feelings and to one another; connecting to the story that is being told, connecting to the person in front of you, and letting that resonate within you.

I am just at the beginning of my learning process as an actor. And this "beginning" is what I want to share with you. My path until now as an actor and experiences. My path and growth as a person.

I had the opportunity to study in an acting school in NYC. I lived four years abroad, having incredible moments, learning how to survive, discovering myself, opening parts of me I didn't even know existed before, feeling joy, sadness, love taking over, passion, pain, compassion, caring, rage… I felt completely alone sometimes, away from my loved ones, tough moments, but I wouldn't change a thing. Because otherwise, I wouldn't be who I am today, I wouldn't have the opportunities I am getting and I wouldn't be writing this book and sharing my experiences if I hadn't risked it all, if I hadn't followed my dreams with faith and determination and faced all the obstacles that came into my path.

Such a long road ahead, but we should never forget why we are where we are now, in the present moment, and how long we've walked to get there. We should never stop learning to appreciate and be thankful for everything that happened and all the lessons learned.

I hope you can connect to it. Not only if you are an actor, not only if you are an artist, not only if you want to live in another country. This book is for all the big dreamers out there, for people who like to travel, for people who appreciate art, for all the people who just maybe like to read stories, autobiographies. I am not a famous actress, I am far away from that, but who knows? Maybe five, 10, 20 years from now, or maybe I will just keep working with what I love and sharing my experiences in these 25 years of my life, now, in this book. That's already a big bonus for me. Maybe in my forties or fifties I will write another one. About my ordinary life.

Welcome aboard.

Acknowledgments

Thanks to all my friends back home, and around the world. Thanks to my family. Geraldo Pedro Linn, Joana Quintana, Maria Isabel Alves de Campos, Cintia Fowlks, Rovena Zanchet, Graça Cristina Campos, Marcelo Campos, Maria Teresa Campos, Maria Teresa Tschiedel, Marina de Campos Brandão, Maria do Carmo Campos, Luiza Eschiletti, Maria Amélia Campos, Maria Inês Campos, Rosa Maria Campos, Paulo Campos, Celso Campos, Zé Campos, Laura Hildebrand Campos, Antônia de Campos Varela, Tatiana Linn, Rodrigo de Marsillac Linn, Jane Linn, Suzana Linn, Muaren Porto, Matheus Linn, Lucas Linn, Thiago Linn, Gabriel Linn, Maria Paulina Alencastro, Manoela Alencastro de Moraes, Renato Abensur, Moyses Abensur, Tricia Abensur, Sirlene Abensur, Georgina Gomes de Figueiredo, for all the support and love always. To my producer and his family: Andre Frauenstein, Elbie Frauenstein, Samuel Frauenstein, Sarina Frauenstein, my director: Darrell Roodt and fellow actors Jamie Bernadette, Luthuli Dlamini, Armand Aucamp, Thandi Puren and the incredible crew of The Furnace: Christianne Bennetto, Pieter Georg Du Plessis, Dino Benedetti, Justus De Jager, Nadia Scott, Julene Paton, Charlotte Tardits, Michele Amaral, Haydn Van Zyl, Angi Boshoff, Halala Sabela, Leon Gerber, Hendre Jacobs and everyone who is part of the team and made this dream come true.

To my dear friends that encouraged me so much through this journey: Clarissa De Gonçalves, Paula Lavratti, Débora Pisigodisnki, Denise Dallas, Paula Pieralisi, Jéssyca Divan, Jéssica Barcellos, Bibiana Nodari Borges, Luiza Moron, Reine Swart, Francesca Dolan, Carolina Bueno, David Thomas, Ana Maria Frota Lisboa Pereira de Souza, Fabíola Bothomé, Estela Piccinini, Juliana Luiza Agostini, Ana Paula Silvani, Carolina Brandão, Paloma Gabriel Cavalheiro, Maite Jover Marset, Tatiana Fagundes Fischer, Michelle Prompt Alvarez, Bruna Fuzetti, Clarissa Reschke Martins, Rafael Stiborski, Dani Heindrich, Natasha Heinz, Luiza Mattos, Bruna Burmeister, Bianca Duarte, Kandice Van Gról, Lívia Adams, Jacob Carstens, Sula Zatelli, Douglas Nunes, Douglas Pereira, Christelle Belinga, Vivian Martins Costa, Helly Elisabeth Bowens Pereira, Darby Bixler, Laura Cardoso Derlam, Caio Riter, Juan Jose Gonzalez-Zuazo Contreras, Hanno Van Wyk, Camila Vergara, Andrea De Niemeyer-Depero, Haley Drago, Aline Fioravanso, Bete França, Marthina Levezon, Yng Lng, Patricia Mears, Renata Mendes, Paula Casanova, Sabrina Monique, Sequoia Davis, Sam Kate Green, Elisa Petry, Rosa Maria Murtinho, Carolina Gross, Cristina Gross, André

Arteche, Deborah Bapt, Aisha N'Jaye, Ana Paula Nunes, Márcia Ferracini, Renata Ferracini, Martha Sittoni, Tuca Padilha, Raissa Peniche, Giovana Rebelatto, Jonas Souza, Maikel Rosa, Daniel Sasso, Nina Schwab, Dani Suzuki, Dani Faria, Daniella Molon Cecchini, Daniel Dos Santos Tomaz, Dani Valente, Ana Stradiotto, Sabrina Barreto, Fabienne Klotz, Ana Luísa Guedes, Júlia Stradiotto, Eduardo Terra Lopes Simch, Alisha Soper, Andreza Teixeira Ribeiro, Marcello D'Azevedo, Neca Santos, Gary Martin, Michelle Knight, Carol Borne, Marina Coelho Hofmeister, Claudia Pickering, Anna Bennett, Kitty Coufal, Taylor Peer, Laura Krebs, Fernanda Schmitt, Carolina Rosa, Aletéia Selonk, Sarka N. Santos, Neli Costa, Ivana Verle, Susan Pilar, Zenon Kruszelnicki, Burke Pierce, Chris Dolman, Barbara Rubin, Chip Killingsworth, Becca Landis McLartis, Sheila Bandyopadhyay, Angela Nahigian, Todd Peters, Jim DeMonic, Chátila Far, Fernanda Kayser Maciel, Gabi Fleck, Sula Zatelli, Flavia Amon, Marc Aden Gray, Lara Bitencourt, Madalena Bitencourt, Carolina Burin, Marcia Ghignatti, Roberta Sant'Anna Volkart, Rose Ganguzza, Patricia Ganguzza, Paula Taiteulbaum, Graziella Calvano Ferst, Rafaela Teló Klaus, Antonio Grolla, Bibiana Picon, Fernanda De Almeida Lewin, Isabella Zanin, Paulo Nascimento, Carminha Beck, Rachel Zapata, Luiziane Brusa da Costa, James Liberato, Lalá Aranha, Elisa Petry, Sara Cicalo, Joana Trindade, Gabriela Jacques da Silva, Lúcia Magnus Marques, Bruna Paranhos, Nelsa Cardoso, Bruno Wasconcellos Roncolato, Leticia Ribeiro, Camila Barbosa,

Lucas Milhomem Valim Ferreira, Jessica Cotton, Jerri Tubbs, Toni Tingle and Erica Bier. My dear therapist who have helped me so much on my journey: Bruna Holst. Also last but very important: To my incredible editor from Mereo Books: Chris Newton, without him this book would never be made.

And all the friends and people that I didn't mentioned but who were such a big part of my journey, and who gave me so much love and support during these 26 years.

Introduction

For the past four years, since I moved from my home town in Brazil to the US, I have had this desire to write a book, an autobiography of my own experiences and thoughts, along with funny and dramatic stories from my ordinary life. However I have never had the courage to actually think it could work out, or that I would be able to express my feelings or pass along some advice for you out there who might be reading it.

My mom said when I told her I was writing a book: "Laura, what? But you are not a writer, you are an actress." I know it sounds harsh, but that was her first reaction. I didn't study to be a writer, but I've always loved reading and writing.

I wanted to share my experiences as an actor so far. I know there's so much ahead of me, so much to learn as an actor, as a person, but maybe some of the things I lived already can click to someone who's reading and help their path, give some light in the way, who knows? But here am I, putting it out there for you.

After I moved to the US, I kept a journal. Every day I would write about my experiences, fun moments and difficulties living abroad. I took all those journals and started reading them one by one, highlighting the moments I thought were more meaningful and then developing them afterwards. So well, here it is, after my notebooks were all joined together. My stories and adventures. My dreams and obstacles. My qualities and flaws. My life written in a book, in which I have put my heart and soul.

I guess I have some things to share about what I've learned so far, and I just hope that you out there can connect to some parts of it. And enjoy the ride with me.

/

Chapter 1

Beginnings

I guess I should start telling a little bit about me. No, I'm not a famous actor, Oscar nominee or anything like that. I'm just a beginner, a working actress who does what she loves the most. It's not about the prizes, it's not about being famous, it's about the job and what you invest in it. The secret I've learned so far is that you should not give up, you should dream big, work your ass off, give 120%, all you've got and put yourself out there, work hard and the results will come. It's about trying, and trying again, and again. Even if you fail 100 times, it's better than the feeling of realizing years later that you shouldn't have given up on the things you wanted so much. So why shouldn't you have high hopes and believe that you are on the right path? You really should.

I am not a famous writer either, and that's not my goal, though I do love writing. I have been writing, and reading, since I was little. But my goal with this book is to share what I've learned so far and my journey as a human being and actress.

My full name is Laura de Campos Linn, but I just use Laura Linn as an actress or to present myself to people. My mom is still kind of mad at me about that, since I am not using her last name, de Campos, which is very Portuguese. Sorry, mom. In Brazil we are used to having two last names, instead of first and middle name.

I was born in this not-so-small but not-so-big city called Porto Alegre ('Happy Harbor', in English). Interesting name, right? It's in the south of Brazil. Our state, Rio Grande do Sul, makes border with two important countries of South America: Argentina and Uruguay. Porto Alegre is close to two of my favorite cities in the world, Gramado and Canela. There's a European vibe there, cozy, cute little houses, coffee shops, best meat and chocolate fondue ever. I give my word on this. And it's also one of the most important touristic points in Brazil. You won't regret it if you go there one day. It's really beautiful and calm. Brazil has tons and tons of beautiful places to visit, and even though people around the world sometimes think it's one of the most dangerous countries – and yes, there's a lot of violence here – Brazil has a unique and positive energy as well, safe places, nature, beauty, culture and our people are known to the rest of the world as a very friendly and welcoming population and considered to be "happy people" in some ways, because we know how to appreciate a simple moment at the beach, or an afternoon with friends and family, and that seems enough to make us happy, chilled and thankful. And you might have heard about the biggest festival in our country: Carnival. I've met so many people abroad, Americans, Europeans, etc that when I say I am from Brazil they all reply: I wish I could go and be there for Carnival. Yes, it's an incredible experience. Specially in Rio de Janeiro. Millions of people in the street, costumes, samba, dancing, joy everywhere. You should put it on your bucket list as a place to visit: Rio de Janeiro, one of the most beautiful cities in the world, and if you can go during Carnival, it's a plus. There's also soccer, which was a big thing for Brazilians and still is, but after we lost in the World Cup 7:1 to Germany, I guess the world's vision about our soccer might have gone differently.

Brazil is also considered to be the richest country in biodiversity. Second biggest reservoir of fresh water in the world, the highest renewable energy potential per square km and the biggest extension of tropical forests in the world. Yes, there's many positive points about Brazil. There are pros and cons, but definitely worth a visit.

My mom told me that when I was four years old I would prepare my backpack and spend the entire week with it, walking around the house from one side to the other, excited to go visit my dad and take my flight to the north of Brazil, where he used to live, a city called Maceió in Alagoas State. Yup. I have been a little adventurer since 1991.

I am ridiculously close to my family, too close even. My mom's family is pretty damn big, eight siblings total. And I have 21 cousins from first degree. True. We are very close though, always trying to make lunch or dinner once in a while to get together, and Christmas and New Year are always a big thing for us. I feel a bit sorry for my cousins who are now grown-ups because they still have to enter the room with the little ones and sing Christmas songs as if they were seven or eight. It's still fun though, for all of us. It's our tradition and after my grandfather died, we sold the house where all our big meetings and celebrations took place, but my aunts Maria Amélia, Graça Cristina Campos and Maria Teresa made sure not to lose our connection and kept doing these events at their houses. My grandpa, Lélio Campos, was one of the biggest inspirations for me and will always be.

They say you don't know life or really appreciate it until you have experienced death, somehow. Not generalizing, but if and when you lose a loved one, someone close to you, it seems that your entire life changes, your visions about life, love, what really matters to you in this world, change. I agree – and I hope that no one needs to lose someone they love to feel this way – because after losing Grandpa, I started to give so much more attention to my surroundings, I started to be more thankful for everything I have, the simple little things and the people I love the most. My family. Eight kids that my grandfather and grandmother, Vininha Campos, had. And it was more common to have a lot of children during the 50s and 60s. But still it's a lot of kids and responsibility, right? Grandpa, even working 10 hours a day as a lawyer, he loved to study anthroposophy and philosophy, listen to Beethoven, play the piano, and read stories to all of us. He could be exhausted, but he always made time for his kids. He was the one dropping them and picking them up at school, he was the one to get them off to sleep and talk to them, giving advice. The most patient guy I've ever known. While my dearest Grandma made sure to be the best wife, mom and always taking care of the house and her loved ones. Doesn't matter how big or small your family is, it's a big gift to be close to one another.

I remember when my Grandpa was around his nineties and we would sit in the living room and read Shakespeare together, since he couldn't see that well anymore, I would sit next to him, hold his hand and read *Romeo and Juliet* or *Othello* and we would discuss it for hours and hours. He was such a huge inspiration for me, and one of the reasons I kept dreaming big and decided to move from our hometown is that I believed he wanted that for me. Once, he told me that I was very sensitive and creative and I needed to use that for something, to share with the world. Little by little, I found what that was. Acting!

I went to high school, the same one, for my entire life, except for one week, short version of this, here we go: I decided to make a move, wanted a change, went to another school, regretted it deeply and came back to my old school, end of story. But those were good times! I miss the breaks for snacks on the patio, our soccer and handball games, although I suck in handball. Seriously, there was this one time that I was the goalkeeper, or *goleiro* as we call it in Brazil, and was freaking out because this huge, strong girl was running towards me and I closed my eyes and prayed, and when I opened them the ball hit my head and I fell to the ground. Lesson learned. Don't you ever close your eyes or pray in the middle of a game, please. Well, I guess no one ever did that, but I'm just putting it out there.

I remember one day coming back from school, and telling my sister: "I want to be a grown-up and work and do stuff that grown-ups do". She looked me in the eye, seriously, and said: "Do not worry because this time will come, and it goes faster than you think, so please enjoy being a teenager and only worrying about math equations, physics, history... it's good times, Laura. Time flies, sis."

I started to go to English School when I was seven or eight years old. For the first or second year I used to hate it, didn't want to go to class, but looking back now, I am so grateful that my mom and dad insisted on me going and studying hard, because even if I don't have the best English and I am still working on reducing my accent, I wouldn't be writing this book in English, and I wouldn't be able to move to the US having already the basics of English language.

The friends I made during my time in high school, Bom Conselho, are still some of my best friends. They were the ones who supported me through one of the most difficult times I had, with more than 10 years of friendship. These people are the family I chose. I can't deny that some of us lost touch, or took different paths, some moved to Australia or London, or somewhere out there in the world, while others are still in our city, Porto Alegre, but the real love and friendship continue. Every time we reunite, it seems like time didn't pass; the affection and caring towards one another is there, alive. And true friendship is one of the greatest gifts we have in life.

Chapter 2

The Scary
Dating World

A great friend of mine, Fernanda Kayser Maciel, said
to me a few months ago: "Laura, your life in general
and your love life are a roller coaster, babe, and it is
OK, because that's how you are, you love people, you
open your heart so much and even though you get hurt
sometimes, I admire you for going and trying." With
the years passing, I am learning to only give to those
who show affection and caring as well and I am trying
to be a little bit more careful and taking baby steps, a

very, very important thing. My essence is still here, I am very honest and I go for it when the subject is relationships and everything else life: trips, work, adventures, etc. I am the first to raise my hand and say: "I am *iiiiin!*"

Oh, man, but I admit my heart was broken in a thousand pieces once, twice, thrice and I cried my eyes out, and healed. With time. We all go through that. We all had our hearts broken at some point, or points, plural. But you fall and you stand up again. "Jump and you'll find how to unfold your wings as you fall" - Ray Bradbury. Don't be sorry for allowing yourself to feel, to cry and to grieve. But also, don't let that become a shadow forever on you. I have had my heart break into pieces, I felt real pain, heart pain, chest pain, I literally felt that I wasn't able to breathe right sometimes. Emotions can cause physical pain, true, but I prefer to feel it all rather than not feeling at all.

One of my exes once said to me once: "Please, Laura, never lose this genuine and dreamy side of you. This pure heart, it's like a child when it's happy, don't let anyone take this out from you, OK?" I won't. Some people run away from "feelings", from talking about stuff, feeling it, and going for it. I don't judge. Everyone has their way of dealing with the matters of the heart or went through things that made them more careful and protective and that isn't bad at all. There's no right or wrong. People have the right to feel how they feel, have their boundaries and respect and love themselves first, above anything else. If someone doesn't like you because of your hair color? You can react the way you want to or not agree, but it's their opinion, their choice. And with this example, I am pretty sure you also wouldn't want to date someone that doesn't want to be with you because of something like that. But you have to respect, buddy. I don't regret saying I live and love fully, with every inch of me, even if I have to pick up my pieces from the floor and put them back together, I know it was worth it, I know I learned something from it with every relationship I had so far, I learned in the toughest way, the hardest way, but a very special person, Eli - someone I will talk about later on - told me recently: "We learn more with our 'unsuccessful' and painful situations than with our successful ones. It can be trite to say that, but it's true, "what doesn't kill you makes you stronger". I still am a hard believer that one day this big dreamy Laura that still has a long way to grow will find her love, will marry, maybe in the mountains or at the beach, just a small ceremony with my family and closest friends. Or at a church, I don't know. The place isn't actually important, just the person out there. But that's me, "nice to meet you" – open to explore, to feel, and be open to love, even if it hurts. A big dreamer. A big lover. I am 26 and will continue to be a dreamer, but maybe with my feet on the ground a bit more and knowing it will never be a fairy tale, I don't want it to be and it won't be, there's no such thing as a perfect relationship. We can't control other's feelings, if it's not reciprocate, it is ok, will hurt like hell, but I do believe everything begins and ends at exactly the right time. And that everything happens for a reason.

In between this crazy dating world with its apps that we live in now, I do have great examples of a true, beautiful, real marriage – my sister and brother in law. And there's plenty of couples out there that are also an example of true love. Joana and Renato are the proof for me that love and companionship still exist and that a marriage can work with dialogue, respect, patience and unconditional love. It's not close to perfect, and it will never be, but it's real and you can see the love and how they care for each other after so many years together. My sister met him in 1994, 23 years ago. That's a pretty damn long time. Something rare to see nowadays. But even before I went back to California (next chapter, wait for it), I always saw from close up how loving and caring they were with one another, respecting each other, and that is gold in a relationship. That's what maintains a real marriage. Passion might not last forever, but love does. Jo always wanted to be a full-time mom and I really admire that.

Being a mom is work, a lot of work. You are a teacher, a mentor to them, you are who they look up to. So she decided to do what she really wanted: to be a mom, be a wife. And after so many years of marriage, having the support of your partner, you should do that, if that's what you want. It is possible, even with all obstacles and daily issues in our lives, to have someone next to us to share our lives with.

I have to say the dating world nowadays is complicated, in my opinion. Because people don't give time to get to know someone, they enter a hundred dating apps and just spend hours staring at their phones: swipe left, swipe right, match. Some talk, some don't. Some people go on the date to meet the person, but they decide by looks, by those pictures on that tiny phone screen. Not everyone, of course not, but from what I hear from friends, colleagues, and see for myself. Maybe we should talk more, get to know the other person, because if there's no connection at all, no chemistry, nothing, then OK, move along. But if there's something, give it another try, because you can't really get to know someone in a one-hour date trying to talk in a loud bar. I know we look at someone, we talk for five seconds and just "know". But honestly? We might be wrong. Trust your guts, yes, but do not also judge someone right away, maybe the person is nervous, and not being herself. Give it some time.

"Don't judge the book by its cover". People want everything now, right now. Specially in big cities like NYC and LA – and I talk about this from my experience and from what I've seen and lived. There are so many "options" out there that people really think that there's someone better. I had a time when I thought like that, so I am not pulling out of this, I experienced that. After breaking up with one of my exes, I went on a few dates, and if it wasn't that good I would say to myself, "Mmm, maybe that other person that matched last night with me on Tinder or OK Cupid or whatever online dating app it was, maybe that person is more interesting". I made mistakes, I really lost the opportunities to make real connections, even if it ended just in friendship. Not "just", because friendship is a true blessing. But that's why I am here saying how important it is to keep it real in this world that is being consumed by technology and its illusions.

I mean, if you see there's a connection but maybe not chemistry, why not go on a second date and see what happens? You mind end up as good friends. It's the "liquid love", as Zigmund Bauman wrote in his book called *Liquid Love: On the Frailty of Human Bonds*. Zigmund wrote: "And the same thing happens in a culture of consumption like ours, in favor of products ready for immediate use, quick solutions, instant satisfaction, results that do not require prolonged efforts, infallible recipes, insurance against all risk and money back guarantees. The promise to learn the art of love is the promise (false, misleading, but inspiring of the deep desire for it to be true) to achieve "experience in love" as if it were any other commodity. It seduces and attracts with its ostentation of those characteristics because it supposes desire without waiting, effort without sweat and results without effort." These are the times we are living in right now. Everything we want is either now or never, we become more and more impatient. Not only on things related to relationships, love, but to everything that surround us. Work, material goods, etc, we want instant satisfaction. We are replacing the quality of a real relationship, things or moments for quantity, and this is not good.

We are who we are, full of flaws along with the qualities, knowing that tomorrow we can be a better version of ourselves, if we want to and put effort in it, because that's what we should always be searching for. We should keep on working to live the life we want and do good. Believe me, things will come to you when you least expect them. But first of all, before anything, you need to love YOURSELF. You need to care deeply for yourself, because if you don't, no one else will.

Chapter 3

Daydream Believer

Oh I could hide 'neath the wings
of the bluebird as she sings
The six o'clock alarm would never ring
But it rings and I rise
Wipe the sleep out of my eyes
The shavin' razor's cold and it stings
Cheer up, sleepy Jean
Oh, what can it mean
to a daydream believer
and a homecoming queen.

Daydream Believer, John Steward, recorded by The Monkees.

This song by The Monkees I used to listen to when I was a child, and I am that big daydream believer. You know those songs that you just want to sing out loud and even when you are sad, they make you smile and warm your heart?

I always loved to go to the movies by myself. Since I was 10 years old, I would go to the nearest shopping mall in my city, close to my house, and see tons of movies. I used to like to sit in the front row and I still do – my neck hurts a bit, but I like to be fully immersed in the movie. If I am going with a friend or family, they just totally hate it, sitting so close to the screen. I feel devoured by the scenes, I feel the butterflies in my stomach every time I go (well, at least when it's a good movie, which doesn't happen all the time). I love the feeling when a movie really moves you so that you carry on until you arrive home, a movie that makes you think or remember a moment of your past or something in the future you would like to happen. Or a feeling that connects to a lover, the loss of a dear someone in your life. Or a movie that makes you want to do something, that gives you a little push in real life. That's what books, movies, songs, plays, art in general and also therapy help me with – this "push", this energy.

My mom and my dad always wanted for me to be a lawyer or a doctor, or something more "stable", I would say. All careers nowadays are tough, but at least they thought there would be an easier path for me. Graduate, get a job, have my own money, buy a house, etc, etc, etc. I don't blame them. I guess when I become a mom I will worry a lot about them and would do anything to protect them. I want them to be happy, though I do believe that you have to do what you love, otherwise you will be miserable. Work takes around 6 to 8 hours of your day or even more, and if you simply hate what you are doing, you won't be happy. Some people don't have a choice to really pursue their dream careers, because you and I and all of us need money, we need to survive. But if you can, at least try to do the things you like, pursue a career that you are passionate about, that will make you improve and keep growing, and if you still end up in a job that you don't like, try to find hobbies, things that will make you excited again and feel alive again.

My mom was more closed off and always had this passion and this dreamy side. She kept her emotions to herself, trying to hide them, but with time they have grown so much inside her that she needs to let it all out. I once told her, when I was about 16 years old (and she always reminds me of that), that all the times she didn't cry, all the tears in her life, all the hugs she didn't give but kept to herself, all came on me. Because I feel that my emotions are my biggest tool, if I truly learn to put them into my work and not everything in my personal life. And lately, she keeps reminding me of what I said, almost 10 years ago, and saying that she wishes she had been more open and that, even at 68 years old, she wants to improve, she wants to change, to let her emotions out. I think it's a wonderful thing. Feel the happiness, feel the sadness, really, truly feel it, and let it all out, cry, smile, laugh. But put it out, don't let all be hidden inside of you, in a prison. To be honest, if I didn't have my career, if I didn't have acting, stories to tell, stories to immerse myself into, I would probably overwhelm the person who is with me, make the person crazy or go crazy myself. I am so thankful that I have this strong emotional side and this love, sensitivity to put into something – into art.

After one, two, three years, while I was still in college, I was trying to convince my parents that I should study film-making. I wanted to explore and see how it felt to be in a movie set, to breathe the art, to feel the crazy but fun atmosphere where everyone is working as an ensemble, running around to make sure everything is in the right place and hear the word 'ACTION!' During these two and a half years at my Bachelor degree in Brazil, I've learned so much about the history of cinema, production, photography. I learned to use Final Cut, a big thing for me. I had incredible teachers there who helped understand the "behind the scenes" world of the movie industry.

By the end of the second semester, I decided that I wanted to do an acting course. As a good Sagittarius, being very adventurous and passionate, I started looking one night on my computer for schools to apply to, scholarships, etc. There were a lot of cities and lots of options: New York, Los Angeles, Atlanta, London... I went to California once, with my dad, in 2006 to do the California Coast road trip, and I fell in love with that place straight away. So, it wasn't that hard to choose. I chose Los Angeles, California. I found this really interesting program at New York Film Academy – an intense acting course for three months. That was it. My mind was made up, and that's where I was going.

It took me a while to convince my parents about it, specially because I didn't finish my university course, but since it was vacations for three months in Brazil, it matched perfectly because this was a short program and would definitely help me to discover why I liked acting so much. My mom was saying "Laura, come on, you already chose the hard path of film-making, and now you want to do acting?" She was terrified, which I understand. I was only 17 years old, moving to a different country, different culture and all of that and doing something completely new. Until they finally supported me in my decision and, a few days after I was on a plane on my way to Los Angeles, by myself.

Thankfully I did have a place to stay. I found this

cozy small apartment in Burbank, far away from everything, but close to my school, NYFA, and close to many movie studios like Disney, Universal Studios, etc. The sensation I was having was weird but in a good way – Fears? Yes, of course, I had many of them and still do, but there was something comforting about being there and it felt right at the time.

TINY DANCER

"... Hold me closer tiny dancer
Count the headlights on the highway
Lay me down in sheets of linen
You had a busy day today..."

- Elton John & Bernie Taupin

There are many songs and movies that I love. I will at least try to do a list of my Top 10 movies. Scenes that I will never forget, scenes that had a big meaning for me, scenes from those movies where I did a monologue or a scene.

OK, top 10, here we go:

I Am Sam, The Hours, Eternal Sunshine of The Spotless Mind, Before Sunrise, Lost in Translation, Brokeback Mountain, Le Fabuleux Destin d'Amélie Poulain, The Bridges of Madison County, La Vie En Rose, and... *Almost Famous*. Each one of these movies had an impact on me, in different ways. That made me understand myself better and develop my love for acting.

"Hold me close, Tiny Dancer, count the headlights on the highway

Lay me down in sheets of linen, you had a busy day todaaaaaay"

This song is the soundtrack #1 of my life - *Tiny Dancer* by Elton John.

I love Almost Famous. Why? Well, I was 13 years old when my sister Jo told me, "Laura, you need to watch this movie," and I was like, "Nah, I don't know." Seemed old – it was released in 2000 and we were in 2004, so no, it wasn't old – I was just being a teenager and the movie was set during the 70s (that's why I felt it was kind of old) and I was just in a phase when I liked to be a rebel and say no to everything. It took me a year to finally say yes and watch it. And it's the first and only movie that I can't explain why I love it. It's a mix of everything with a touch of magic. There are beautiful scenes, and the story is about this young journalist who has a chance to write to *Rolling Stone* magazine about this band during the 70s, "Stillwater". It's a semi-autobiographical story, since Cameron Crowe, the director, was also a teenage writer for *Rolling Stone*. However, there's a touch of magic in this movie. There's a unique energy. It's a movie I can see 200 times, and I swear I've already watched it at least 30 times. It brings me a sense of adventure, love and broken hearts, dreams, music and the scene where they are all in a bus, mad at each other, and *Tiny Dancer* starts to play, it's like I am part of that. I start singing with them and all the fear, the stress, the real life disappears for those four, five minutes. Music can change our moods, our lives.

Tiny Dancer even became my graduation song, when I graduated in film-making in Brazil. Of course, there's a big list of songs I like, but this is the one for me. Even though I have loved going to the movies since I was nine, ten years old, this movie was a "boom", made my heart explode, and even at 14 years old, close to the end of high school, I knew that I wanted to work with movies. Didn't know where, what part of the crew I would like to be, behind the cameras or in front of them, but I knew that's where I belonged.

I'm talking a lot about theatre and acting, movies and dreams. But it's all connected to life, and passion and love. I guarantee you. Even if you are not an actor, maybe you do like movies. I still don't know you, but you know me a bit already and you'll learn more in the next chapters.

Chapter 4

NYFA, Dawson's Creek and Michelle Williams

Classes started mid-December of 2009, at the New York Film Academy in Los Angeles. I know, it's kind of weird they call it NY Film Academy and it's in LA, but OK, they just expanded to other cities and kept the name. I was so nervous on my first day of school, but excited, too. It's amazing how we connect with some people right away. I made some amazing friends from day one and now, after seven years, we still keep in touch. Anna Bennett, Claudia Pickering, Reine Swart, Jacob Carstens, Helly Elizabeth Bowens, Haley Drago, and the list goes on, but those people really stayed with me. It doesn't feel it was so many years ago, I still remember like it was yesterday, our classes together, the fun times, the best club sandwich in the world right downstairs at the coffee place. We used to have classes in the morning, afternoon and night. We were simply immersed in the world of acting. And it was incredible! We had amazing teachers as well, like David Robinette, Adam Nimoy, Susan Kent...

Susan. I will never forget our first day of class. We were all introducing ourselves to the others and we did an exercise where she randomly chose two people to sit in front of each other. We had to look into each other's eyes and after we made a truthful connection, some of us had to say something like "you are needy", and if the person sitting in front told you that and you felt she was reading your heart, you would only need to repeat "I am needy", and then you had to make an observation about her or him. But if you didn't agree with what the other person said you could just give it back and say "you are needy". It's better doing it than explaining, of course, but what I am trying to share here is how transparent you have to be as an actor. You are there, completely naked on the inside, opening up yourself, your feelings and your soul. Let the feelings in and out. Let others touch the deepest part of you.

At the end of that exercise I was feeling so emotional, but so relieved, too. And at the end of that class she said: "In these three months you will know these people here, in this room, better than you know anyone else in your life". She was right! Some of those friends/classmates are still my friends now, after eight years, and to see their beautiful journey and all they achieved so far is amazing. Some became directors, others kept on in the acting direction and some went to a completely different profession, but all of us know how those months inside that building made us stronger and more sensitive. Only we know what we went through together, what it was like to have a naked soul and having to share your deepest fears and emotions.

Those three months in LA in 2009/2010 were so meaningful to me and made me grow so much, giving me more focus and maturity. They also gave me the certainty that I wanted to pursue acting. But a very unfortunate event happened in the middle of this beautiful time at NYFA. My appendix was about to... explode! The appendix is considered not to be useful. Dear appendix, at least you gave me a funny-tragic story which I can tell my grandkids one day.

After graduation there at NYFA, I still had one or two months to stay in the USA. I was determined to stay in LA, but I knew that I needed to go back to Brazil and at least finish my graduation in Film-making. Unluckily enough, two weeks before I was due to come back to Brazil I had appendicitis. Not a cool thing. For those who've had it, you know the pain. I was walking home from the coffee shop with a friend of mine and was feeling very nauseous and with a lot of pain in my stomach, but I thought it was only cramps or something. I got home and lay in bed for a while but the pain became stronger and stronger and when I tried to get out of bed, I literally fell on the floor.

Immediately I talked to my friend and said: "We need to go to the hospital, like, right now".
OK, we finally got there. They put me on a stretcher and did tons of tests and examinations. I still remember the nurse saying: "Worst case scenario you have appendicitis and we'll need to operate straight away." The doctor came back with the exam results and said: "You need to have surgery now." I was in panic, didn't know what was going on and the worst part of it all was that beside my friend/roommate, I was by myself, no family to help, nothing. And I was only 18 years old. It wasn't such a big deal but it was still risky.

I had to do the surgery immediately because my

appendix was about to explode. Imagine that, a general infection in my body, no no no, not cool. I called my mom and my dad, and they were terrified as well, wanting to come and stay with me, my dad even had to give a pill for my mom to calm down, but there was one person that I considered family and was an angel – still is – in my life – Cintia Fowlks.

She went to the hospital and stayed there the whole time. When I entered the surgery room, I remember being in the stretcher with my arms wide open and locked, I literally looked like Jesus Christ on the cross. I wasn't hallucinating or anything, but I looked to my right side and there he was, my doctor, with his mask, sitting down, praying with his eyes closed and there was an opera song playing. I felt as if I was in a movie, but not a comedy one, or drama, more likely a thriller/horror movie.

I closed my eyes and said: "Well, if I don't get out of this one, thank you God for 18 wonderful years of experiences and please take care of my family and friends." I opened my eyes and looked at my left side and there was the nurse. I asked her, "When am I going to fall aslee…" *boom.* All I remember afterwards was waking up (thankfully), opening my eyes and everything was kind of blurry, but I was alive, still on lots and lots of pain killers and morphine, yes, but I knew I was alive. As my friend, who is a psychoanalyst, once said, this type of medication for extreme and severe pain is sometimes so strong that it takes away your emotional pain. And it's been proved that feeling anxious, sad or heartbroken causes real pain. You might end up in a hospital thinking you are having a heart attack (you are not), but our emotions are deeply connected to our bodies.

Anyhow, they took me to my room, and I felt sleepy and dizzy for hours and hours. And pain, yes, lots. But the morphine was the good part of it. I felt like my body was an amoeba, all melting, no pain, just sleepy. I never went to the drug side too hard. I drink socially, and I used to smoke cigarettes, but thankfully I got rid of that addiction this year. Weed? I tried a few times and it didn't work well for me, but besides those three, nothing. And morphine, on this occasion, yes. In the artistic world specially, you are surrounded by options and people offering you drugs, and thankfully I never wanted to go there, but I didn't ask for the morphine – the doctor gave it to me – so I don't feel bad at all about trying. It was a nice, a very nice, experience.

I was so thankful that I had so many great friends that visited me there. It was hard to be so far away from home, from my family and loved ones, but I had some amazing people out there to help me. Cintia, my best friend and the most amazing human being I've ever met, took me to her house to stay with her after the days at the hospital, where she held my hand the entire time. I wanted to stay in California, but I knew I had to go back to my country, finish my grad school in film-making first, then I could go wherever I wanted, after I graduated.

Oh, Michelle Williams. Part of the title of this chapter and a reason why. Beautiful, stunning, incredible Michelle Williams! Before my appendicitis, at the end of the program at NYFA we needed to prepare a scene or monologue that would be screened at a theatre in Hollywood as our graduation. I did one of my favorite monologues back in that time and that still is one of my favorites. The monologue I chose is from the TV Show *Dawson's Creek*, where the character Jen Lindley (Michelle Williams) records a video while she's in hospital for her baby girl, who's only a year old. Jen is sick and could die at any moment, so she wants to say important things for her girl, what she wishes for her, what really matters in life. That monologue still touches me so much, because it's says everything about love, life and how we should be thankful for what we have in our lives.

This is how the monologue goes (a part of it):

"Hi, Amy, it's mom... I thought I should give you a little list of the things that I wish for you. Well, there's the obvious. An education. Family. Friends. And a life that is full of the unexpected. Be sure to make mistakes, make a lot of them, because there's no better way to learn and to grow, all right? And then there's love. I want you to love to the tips of your fingers, and when you find that love, wherever you find it, whoever you choose, don't run away from it, but you don't have to chase after it either. You just be patient, and it'll come to you, I promise, and when you least expect it..."

As I wrote down this monologue, I already felt the butterflies in my stomach, the emotion coming from inside me and how beautiful and meaningful this all means. It's sad, of course, but also full of beauty and light. This monologue says so much about me, as well. I see myself in her, how she feels, and these would be my words to my daughter if one day I passed away too early and could not see her grow. Michelle Williams is definitely one of my inspirations as an actress. *Dawson's Creek* really inspired me to become an actress, to follow my dreams. One of the reasons I went to Film School in Brazil was because I saw Dawson's passion for movies, writing, his room full of posters of Steven Spielberg movies.

And talking about Michelle Williams, jumping more than seven years from the time I did the monologue, I actually had the opportunity to meet her. I went to see *Cabaret* on Broadway in NYC, while I was studying there. She absolutely amazed me with her performance and seeing her live was a blessing. At the end of the show, lots of people, including me, were waiting in line outside, freezing (it was winter), to say hi and ask for an autograph. After a long wait, I saw her coming outside with a huge smile on her face and being sweet with everyone. Then there she was, in front of me, and I was nervous and speechless. She gave me her autograph and there was this big security guy next to her, twice her size. Some hidden courage came out of me and I said: "You are one of the reasons why I decided to study theatre and become an actor." She smiled and said: "Really, why?" And I replied: The first monologue I've done was from your show, *Dawson's Creek*." She said: "Which one?" and smiled. Then I started saying the words from the monologue, looking at her eyes, with all my love and caring, and she was looking back at me with tears in her eyes and a smile. I asked her if I could take a picture with her and before she replied, the big man, the security guy said: "No. No pictures allowed." Michelle looks at him and says: "Yes, I will take a picture with her". We took the picture, I gave her a hug and she went away.

I'm sharing this story not to show off, at all. For me, this story is about inspiration and how we are all humans, doesn't matter if you are famous or not, rich or poor, we all have emotions and I won a huge present that night, I made a true connection and touched somehow a soul, that of one of my favorite actresses. I went home freezing outside but inside I was warm enough after this loving and unforgettable moment.

Chapter 5

The Graduate

No, I'm not talking about the movie *The Graduate* with Dusting Hoffman, which is pretty amazing, but the life of a graduate. In 2010, I came back to Brazil, to my home sweet home, Porto Alegre. It took me a while to adapt again. Of course I was super happy being around my family and friends and my little niece, who was born to my dear sister on May 6th 2010. She was, is and always will, be the light of my life. I know I am not a mother yet, but being a godmother and an auntie is such a precious gift. I spend days and days at my sister's and brother-in-law's house taking care of that sweet little girl. It was the place I felt really home, being by their side. And also with my mom.

But the city, Porto Alegre? I have never felt home there. Except for the fact that I was with my family and friends, the city itself didn't make me feel like I was home. Only the people. I do think all of us belong somewhere, or we have that feeling that there's a place in the world we feel at home, completely. Like we belong. Places that maybe we haven't even visited. There's just a feeling, a certainty if you may call it that. California was that place to me, at that time.

Well, now I was finishing my graduation at film-making. It was the craziest semester ever, because we decided to put all the class together and actually do a feature movie, instead of making little groups, and each one would make a short film, 5-10 minutes. I thought it was a great idea, but, oh man, it was so chaotic and such a mess, specially at the beginning, to put everyone together and all the ideas and try to agree what we were going to do. Hours and hours of brainstorming, trying to figure out what the story would be about. It was like five short movies together, connected. We had five or six directors and only 15 days to shoot everything. Lots of struggle, but we were able to make it. I was the assistant director and also the editor. Editing a movie with five directors sitting next to you wanting the piece they directed to show more? Tough job. There was a lot of ego talking, wanting to show, but for two, almost three months I spent every day in the office at our university, editing. The results were good, better than we expected. The name of our movie was *5 Ways To Close Your Eyes*. The stories really linked to one another. We were proud of our work together and working as an ensemble, even with the difficulties, we made it work.

We were a happy graduation class, and we achieved our goal, though it wasn't perfect, of course. The editing could and always can be better. I think editing is like writing a script or a book, because so much changes when you edit a movie. You can simply create another story, you can see the scenes and put them in a different order, change the pace, create a rhythm to it. That's why I love editing so much. And, if I wasn't still confused at the time and had my guts telling me that acting was what I wanted to do for the rest of my life, I would definitely have chosen this path, being an editor for films, TV series, etc. It's an art.

I will never forget the days we filmed in the middle of the streets of Farrapos in Porto Alegre. I will never forget when we filmed inside a party house called Cabaret that doesn't exist anymore, well, not at that place, at least, because months later it was burned down. But those are memories I will carry with me and all I've learned in school helped me to become a better actor, for sure, and to really understand what happens inside a set, being the boom guy, the assistant, the continuity supervisor, etc etc etc. And how each person working on a set is unique and important. We are a team and a movie or a play can only happen if we work together, as an ensemble. I learned how to deal with some hard people, people with egos, and also with a lot of amazing and kind people.

And then, finally, graduation came: check. But what now? My head was spinning, so many thoughts and doubts. What am I going to do? Where am I going to find work in my field? Is this really what I want to do for the rest of my life? I guess all of us can relate to these questions, because it doesn't matter what field you work in, the world outside is scary. Even if studying, tests, exams are difficult when you are graduating, somehow it feels like a safe place. I had been fearless about so many things in life, traveling etc, but now I was so damn scared.

So I started looking for jobs, and thankfully my movie production teacher got me a great opportunity to work at a film production company. I was there for three months maximum, but I learned a lot about production, producing films, organizing tons of paperwork, making calls, making sure everything was on time. One of my best friends, Clarissa de Gonçalves, was working with me and she is one of the people I look up to. She has such a strong willpower, so focused and determined. We lived five blocks away from each other, so we would always come back home after work together.

But it was time for me to move on, find another job, because producing wasn't what I wanted. I was able to contact a book editing company, a very well-known company in Brazil, specially for those tiny pocket books you can take with you everywhere. I worked there as a producer for their website videos, interviews, etc. I interviewed great writers from our city and had the chance to talk to them, to understand more about the world of writing, fiction writers, poetry writers. And I had an incredible boss and writer, Paula Taitelbaum.

But still, something was missing. The work, the city I was in, a whole inside of me. They say it's not the place you are in that will make you happy, and I agree. But I do think it's part of it. To be in a place that you feel good, just being there, existing.

My mom, Balala Campos (her artistic name – when she was little, she made a drawing and the first words she wrote was "Balala", so my grandparents started to call her that) has had a journalism company for more than 16 years, a communication advisory company to be more precise. I have such respect and admiration for the effort and courage my mom has and how much she puts her heart into her work. She was also a single mom, needing to juggle with being a journalist (during the 70s and 80s it wasn't such a well-paid job) and building her career, her own business and also take care of Jo, providing a good and stable life for both of them. My sister Joana is a strong woman, and she has been my hero all my life. She lost her dad when she was only a teenager, and even before he died, he wasn't present in her life. She went through hard moments, but she managed the best way she could, while studying Social Communication - Advertising at the University, she started to work really early, owning around R$300 (Reais) which is equivalent to less than $100 nowadays. Even with such a small salary, she started therapy because our mom couldn't pay. And she did that because she knew that it was important to her, to deal with her past, to understand the present situations in a better way and to create a future of her own and what she really wanted: A family. More than anything. Maybe she wanted that so much because that wasn't the example she had at home. She wanted the opposite of what she had lived. She wanted a big loving family. And she did achieve her goal. Jo and I have a 16-year age difference. She was like a mom to me as well. She took care of me when I was a baby, I might not remember a great amount of that time because I was so little, but I am sure that the love and appreciation I have for her are so big because of all the tenderness and love she has given me since I was born. She's protective of those she cares for and loves.

My mom and my sister worked together for 10 years. Imagine that, mom and daughter, working together for that long. Sometimes working with family can work, sometimes not. But my mom and sister are very, very different in a lot of ways. My sister is more of a perfectionist, wanting to do everything right, paying attention to detail, and my mom doesn't pay attention to detail that much, she is great at what she does but she likes to do it in her own way, so they both worked by themselves, kind of, trying to communicate the important things, but each with a separate office.

Everyone has their own way, and it's tough to change. True willpower is needed. You have to change your habits, change your behavior, but if you can do it, it's for your own good. And also for the ones who are around you. We need to be more flexible for things to flow in a better way.

I thought to myself after a while, why not try to work with them? It was related to my field, I liked working with social media too, and their clients could definitely need help with promo videos and things like that. We also got a secretary, a few months after I entered the company, so it was four people, in a tiny space. But it wasn't working well. To be truly honest,

I wasn't doing so well, either. I was always carrying the feeling that I needed to leave Brazil again, I still felt locked in there. Ask any Sagittarius what they think of that, not having their freedom, and whether you believe in astrology or not, they probably will tell you, no, I do not like pressure or not having my freedom. Some people like to work eight, ten hours in front of the computer, but some people just can't keep their butts in a chair for that long.

I remember as if it was yesterday when I sat down with my mom and sister and told them I wanted to leave the company. I worked there for almost two years total, from the end of 2011 until 2013. January 2013 was when I said: "Mom, please don't take this badly, I know how much you wanted for us to keep going with your company, but I am not happy here, at all. I want to travel again, I want to go back to California. So, I hope you'll support me, but if not, I am leaving the company anyway."

That was a shock to my mom. She was speechless. Somehow having us both around was a certainty, she had counted on us taking care of the work after she retired or something. She is always very worried about money, which we all are but at different levels. Then, two or three days later, talking to my sister, she made the same decision: to leave the company. I think I kind of helped her to finally make this decision. She wasn't happy working 8-9 hours a day and still having so little time with my niece Mari, who was three years old now. My dear sister Joana is that type of person who was born to be a mom, and all she ever wanted was a family, a happy and loving family. Not the TV commercial type of happy, but a real one, with concerns and difficulties, but with two people who really want to stay together and raise their kids, and travel, and take care of each other. And that is her decision, her happiness. That's what she needed to follow.

You probably guessed that I kind of like astrology, since I talked about being a Sagittarius a few times. I truly do. Jo, my sister, is a Scorpio, a strong sign. They are so loyal and faithful to the ones they care about, but don't you ever betray their confidence, don't you ever cheat on them, otherwise you are screwed.

It normally takes a long time for her to speak up and say what she desires, but she finally found the courage to say it. She did it. And I was so proud of her. I wasn't happy to see my mom upset, thinking she wouldn't be able to continue her company without us, but she did and the company still goes on now, even four years after we left. She now works from home, with a home office to look after her clients. At 68 years old she still works her ass off and she loves her work. It's not easy, but I promise her every day that I will make enough money one day and help her out.

After I left the company, I was researching places to study, to do a post-graduation. I even considered Barcelona, Spain. I found a great graphic design and social media program and thought that if I did it, it would help me to help my mom if one day I came back to the company. But something felt wrong inside me, a feeling, an instinct that it wasn't the place nor the career I wanted to pursue. It's one thing to like something, another to want to do that for the rest of your life, as a profession.

So I started researching courses related to acting. UCLA (University of California, Los Angeles) had great ones. I was torn between the Acting program or the Entertainment Studies. I didn't want to disappoint my entire family, since I graduated in Brazil in film-making, by wanting to go straight to acting, so I went for the Entertainment Studies because it had classes in acting, producing, screenwriting, directing, all together. And in that way I could really "discover" what I wanted to do.

Chapter 6

West Coast, East Coast

March 2013 I flew back to California, to start the one-year program. Classes were only at night, starting around 6 or 7 pm until 10, 11 pm. What did I do in my spare time – all day? Well, I worked in the catering department at UCLA. Sometimes I would wake up at 3 am to be at the university at 4 am to start preparing the food, the tables, putting everything on the trucks to the place where the event would be. And after the event finished, we all needed to go back to the base –

the kitchen – and clean everything. It was such a different experience for me, running around like crazy, getting yelled at by the ones that were organizing each event, sounds of plates breaking, dishwashing machines, getting my hand burned because I took the clean plate too soon to put it back in its place. It was an interesting experience for me. I definitely needed the money and I was happy that I found a job, even being a foreigner, that I could work in campus, and help pay the bills. I had some terrible bosses in there. Like, mean, really mean. A horror movie, even. There was this man who would treat us like we were nothing. Even if we did everything he asked, it was never enough. He always wanted to make us feel bad, leave the events crying and feel terrible about our work.

Once I remember that I was putting ice inside the container, it was my second or third day there, and he simply came to me, got the container and dropped all the ice on the floor and said: "Do it again, this time quicker." Then he simply turned his back and walked away with a smile on his face. I am not kidding. My face was all red, I was so angry but at the same time so hurt. How could treating people like shit make you proud and smile? How can people be so mean by choice? Honestly. But I learned an immense lesson. It's like when someone offers you a gift and you refuse it, who stays with the present? The person who offered you. Lesson? Don't let other people's energy affect you in a bad way; what doesn't serve you, do not take it. Bad energies, other people's problems that people throw at you like it was your fault. Simply don't. Let it go in one ear and out the other. Only accept things that will make you grow. Of course you should take responsibility for the mistakes you've made, but the rest, no. So it really made me stronger. I was grateful to have worked in there, and I made true friends, Michelle Prompt, Paula Pieralisi, Bruna Fuzetti, Nina Schwab, that are still such good friends to me and helped me so much while I was living in LA, I had fun moments, between the chaos and nightmares. I left that place with more self-love and belief.

Classes: I was overwhelmed with joy at being taught by such great people, people who worked in the Hollywood business, learning about the pre-production process, screenwriting, production, editing and distributing. There's so much content and material to work on and know. Just the distributing part is huge, how to make the contacts, how to sell your movie, how to get sponsors, executive producers to help your movie to get made. I had to buy more than 10 books to learn more. I had more than 200 pages written about each class, and I still keep those in my bedroom, so that one day I can read them all over again, if I need specific information. Oh, and UCLA Campus is just beautiful.

Go UCLA Bruins. I felt I was in a teenage American movie, one of the ones I used to watch while adolescent.

So I enrolled into acting classes, scene study, monologue, and others. That's where I fell in love and knew 100% that was what I wanted to do. Marc Aden Gray, my acting teacher, was my great mentor in acting. He was the guy that believed in me, the guy that said: "Laura, you need to pursue this, go further, you have what you need".

I started doing private classes with him, to prepare my monologues for the big moment: the audition to enter the American Academy of Dramatic Arts, the school I've always wanted to study at since I was little. Here's a letter I received from him, after we finished school. (See next page).

Letter of
Dramatic Reference

What is a Dramatic Reference

We truly appreciate your time. Your letter of reference is an extremely important part of the admissions process, so we ask you to take a moment and fill out this form today.

The Academy requires one letter concerning dramatic ability. This letter may be written by a member of a high school or college theatre department, or by a director, producer, or other professional theatre person who has had an opportunity to appraise the applicant's potential. Applicants who have had no dramatic training or experience should substitute a second letter of personal reference.

Applicant's Name _____Laura_____Linn_____
First   Last

Dramatic Reference:

Please write a statement of recommendation for the applicant listed above (use second page of this form if necessary) and mail or email this form as soon as possible. Your prompt response will allow us to provide the applicant with a faster admission decision. **Thank you!**

Reference's Name _____Marc Aden_____Gray_____
First   Last
Email Address ___marcadengray.ucla @ gmail·con____ Relationship to Applicant ____Teacher_____

Letter of Dramatic Reference:

To whom it may concern,

I recently had the pleasure of teaching Laura Linn in my UCLA summer semester, Acting Fundamentals.

Laura is without doubt one of the most gifted students I have had in my time at UCLA.

She possesses two qualities (among many) critical for any actor:

Dramatic Reference for: _Laura Linn_   **Page 2**

a fluid emotional life and a powerful reservoir of empathy that she brings not only to her acting but also to her dealings with those around her.

Laura displayed an excellent work ethic in her time with me; she was always prepared, took adjustment and instruction with ease and was hungry to work and experiment in every class.

While working within a framework based on process, it's also worth noting that Laura achieved powerful results. Her scenes and monolog set the standard for our class.

I am delighted to know Laura is seeking further training; many actors with her ability are content to "wing it". Laura has shown a desire to continue learning and evolving as an actress and will add tremendous value to your school. I recommend her with absolute confidence.

Kind regards,
Marc Aden Gray
323. 572. 4911

MAIL TO:
Admissions Office
The American Academy of Dramatic Arts
1336 N. La Brea Avenue
Los Angeles, CA 90028
Or if you prefer, email this form to **LAdocuments@aada.edu**

With his recommendation letter and all his classes, I finally had the chance to audition for the school.

I drove to the school and thankfully a great friend of mine was there, in the waiting room, to hold my hand. I remember I couldn't stop shaking, I was so nervous. It's good to be nervous for an audition, that shows that you care about it, you know? One of my teachers said that once, if you aren't a little nervous about an audition, or the seconds before you enter a scene or the stage, something is definitely wrong. Being a bit nervous shows that you care about what you are doing. Those butterflies are part of what we do, and they bring us energy and adrenaline, but of course, being too nervous, getting to a point where you forget lines or simply have a panic attack, then, no, not good. You have to find a balance. Trust in your work, what you did and worked hard on in your character and play/movie, and then just feel those goosebumps and go for it.

We did a tour first around the school. The LA Campus was newer than the one in New York City. I loved the energy there, the classrooms, the library, their own theatre where they presented the plays done by the students. I can still hear the voice of the woman who called "Laura Linn, you are next". I held my friend's hand so tight, and walked into the room. It was just one teacher/director who would judge my performances and talk to me. Usually they had two or three in the room for that, but not that day. If that is a fortunate or unfortunate thing, I don't know. But that's what I had, and the woman was very nice. She saw I was nervous, as most are, but she helped me to calm down a bit.

I did two monologues, one contemporary and one classic. The classic one was from *Brighton Beach Memoirs*, a drama piece by one of my favorite playwrights, Neil Simon. The contemporary one was from *Bad Habits*, written by Terrence McNally, a comedy piece. She told me, "Don't look at me, because I need to observe your performance, I need you to look into the wall and imagine who you are talking with".

I did the two monologues, but I felt I was too anxious and it didn't go so well. We always judge our own work, but we know, as actors, when we are connected or not. She looked at me and stayed quiet for a while, then she handed me this play *Our Town* by Thornton Wilder, one of the most important American plays of all time. She said, "Sit down there and read this page, we are going to do a cold reading, OK? You have five minutes to read and understand the character and situation and then we will do it".

I was shaking, I was thinking to myself: what am I going to do? Is she asking me to do this cold reading because she thinks I might have potential but wasn't able to show it? No clue. So I tried to let go of the thoughts and focus on the monologue. I read it, stood up and started the monologue. Twenty seconds later she stopped me and said, "I want you to really look into the wall and imagine someone you love deeply, and then repeat with me, 'I love you, I'll miss you, but I have to go now, OK?'" All I can tell you is that after doing that, and imagining my sister on that wall, imagining saying goodbye to her, all my emotions came out from deep inside of my heart and soul. I was bursting into tears, I was connected, I wasn't thinking about what I was going to say, I was just saying to her, with all my love and caring and sadness to leave her.

After the monologue, she smiled and said, "Sit down a bit". I took a while to cool down and come back to earth. She said, "Laura, I wanted to see what I thought you had inside of you, and you do have it all, you were just too nervous to do it. But you did. On my side, you are approved to be part of our school. I just need to talk to my other partners at the school board and in a week or two you will receive a call from us".

I was so happy, I couldn't believe it. Even if I didn't get the chance to study there, I had done my part, I had forgotten the world outside and connected fully to that moment. And that was enough, for that day. I became a better actor, and tomorrow would come and I would keep on trying.

Five days after the audition, I was in IKEA buying things with my roommate for our apartment in LA, and I heard my phone ringing and written on the phone screen was 'AADA' (American Academy of

Dramatic Arts). I dropped everything on the floor, everything I was holding to buy, and answered. A woman said: "Laura, we would like to welcome you to our school, you were approved to be part of the American Academy of Dramatic Arts, congratulations."

I couldn't even speak right. All I could say was "Thank you, thank you, thank you so much!" I was jumping around and screaming at IKEA like a crazy person, not caring what others would think. My friend, Bruna, hugged me and said: "Congratulations, girl, you deserved it."

My dream was coming true, for real. Didn't feel real yet, it felt I was still dreaming. But it was true. I kept repeating it to myself, but I think I spent two days not believing that I had been accepted at the school of my dreams. I called my mom, my dad, my sister, my closest friends to tell them the news and they were all so happy and proud of me. And I take this as one more lesson: When you really want something with all your heart, you can do it. You need to pursue it, to persist, to focus, to give your effort, because, yes, there are the lucky ones, opportunities that appear for people out of nowhere, but that's rare. If you have a bit of talent, tons of determination, focus and you really, really, really want something, go for it. Make your contacts, do your researches, talk to people, engage, dream big, work your ass off, and live day by day as if it was your last one. Risk it. Give your 120%. Because we never know what tomorrow will bring, but we can live the now and give the best version of ourselves to achieve what we want, always being humble and caring. And you will see, you will get there. Sooner or later.

I was one of the few Brazilians that got accepted at the American Academy of Dramatic Arts, where such talented and classic actors as Grace Kelly (class of 1949), Spencer Tracy (1923), Lauren Bacall (1942), Robert Redford (1959), Anne Bancroft (1950), Kim Cattrall (1974), and Danny DeVito (1966) graduated. And more recently, Paul Rudd (1991), Jessica Chastain (1998), Adam Scott (1993) and Anne Hathaway (specialized training 1993). It was a huge opportunity and I couldn't be more thankful to be taught by wonderful teachers and know that so many artists that I admire also went there.

The shock of reality soon knocked on my door: money. How would I be able to pay for this school? It's not cheap, not at all. I applied for one of the scholarships and I was able to get a great amount out of it to help with the expenses from the school, but since I was a foreigner I couldn't try a loan or something.

I guess it's time to talk more about my dad, Geraldo Pedro Linn, the best person I know, the biggest heart

I've ever seen, not only because he's my dad, but because of what he does to others, how much he helps others with needs, and he always, always stood by my side.

He was apprehensive too, about the school and so much money, but he said: "Kid, we will find a way, don't worry." He took some of the money he had in his savings, he made loans in Brazil, all of that to help me survive there and to pay the school upfront (the entire year). My mom also helped as well as she could.

I wanted to visit the school in New York City. I had been to NY in the New Years of 2006 and 2007 with my dad, but didn't remember much. So I went there with my great friend Ana Paula Silvani for a week or two. We had so much fun there, but we also crossed the limits some nights, going to parties and bars. We were amazed by the city and how many things it had to offer (including drinks).

One of those days we woke up so, so hung over. We didn't want to waste the sunny day and miss enjoying our time there, but we were still drunk I guess, we couldn't even think – I am serious. We sat in a coffee shop and for two hours, I mean, literally two hours, we were just sitting there. Even to write a message to our friend took 30 minutes. Our brains were dead, but, as two good, adventurous, crazy Sagittarius girls we kept on going and even had one more drink that night. We were in New York, baby! And every second was worth it, but when we got back to LA, at least from my side, I know I slept an entire day and night to recover.

Going back to the school thing, when I entered those doors in that AADA building I was sure I belonged there. Even though California felt like home, I knew that for my studies and craft in acting, studying in NYC would give me more. Los Angeles and New York City are complete opposites. California, in general, has more of a chilled vibe. Los Angeles is a bit more hectic, a lot of traffic, but it also has the beaches and sun every day, it's rare for it to rain there. In the winter, it's not like NYC, a simple hoodie in LA will keep you warm. NYC is tough and kind of heavy in a way. They call it "the city that never sleeps", and that's true. People work and work and work, and then go to bars with friends to relax after a long day. The transportation is easy, you can get a train, the subway to Brooklyn, Queens, from the top of the island, Bronx to Tribeca in 20-30 minutes ride. You can walk the whole of Manhattan if you want to. It's easy to get around. I didn't want to leave LA, because I made a lot of friends there, true friendships, but it was a great opportunity to live in another city, completely different, and I always loved adventures, so it was one more to my journey.

So I bought my tickets a month before the classes

started. I could transfer from LA Campus to the NY Campus. So I took my flight to the east coast with nothing but one piece of luggage and a backpack and my dreams.

I didn't know many people in Manhattan, just Tricia Abensur, the sister of my brother-in-law, who became family to me. I took care of her kids from time to time and she helped me a lot, recommending me to her friends to babysit as a side job, to help to pay the bills. Fabienne Klotz and Andrea De Niemeyer-Depero were two more friends I made. It was such a pleasure to take care of their kids and I am forever thankful for the love and warm welcome they gave me, and specially the kids, I love children, I definitely want to be a mom one day. I missed my niece every single day, so being around those sweet girls was really good and fun and I felt surrounded by love.

If I can make it there, I'll make it anywhere
It's up to you, New York, New York
New York, New York…
I want to wake up in a city that doesn't sleep…

- from New York, New York, by John Kander & Fred Ebb, recorded by Frank Sinatra in 1979.

The city that never sleeps, the city that has more than eight million people, living, working, 24/7. Instead of cars and highways as I was used to in LA, there was people traffic around the streets. Times Square, all those lights, all those digital screens and billboards, all those people taking pictures, tourists everywhere. The NY skyscrapers, Empire State Building, Rockefeller Center, it was all new and beautiful and scary at the same time. New York is multicultural and more than 36% of its population are foreign-born, one of the highest among US cities. The metropolitan area is home to the largest Jewish community outside Israel. The feeling of being around so many different cultures and people made me feel alive.

They say people in NYC are rude, but I completely disagree. First of all, because we cannot generalize, and second of all, they are just busy with their own lives and problems. But when you do need help and you are polite, you will certainly find caring people who will help you. Once I was kind of lost and asked seven different people around the streets where BH store was, and the answer from all of them was "Sorry, I'm not from NY either." The eighth person I asked was able to tell me, because he was from New York.

This is just to give you an idea how many people from abroad come to NY to try a better life, or are just visiting the "city that never sleeps". I was lucky to have this chance to live there and study. That was 2014.

I spend days and nights doing web searching on AirBnB, Craigslist, groups on Facebook, for a place to live and fortunately I found a Brazilian, Didi Mello, who that had a small room to offer and for a quite good price, compared to most NYC rents. It was in East Harlem, on 106th Street. It was very important for me to have someone who spoke the same language as me, same type of culture and behavior, and she became like a mom to me. She used to cook, and we used to sit on the dinner table and talk a lot, share our stories, our fears. This is a struggle that many people that move to NYC have, find an affordable place to live. It's an expensive and tough city.

I was excited to start school, and also excited because a great friend of my sister, Paula Lavratti, was there with me to visit with her friend Rovena Zanchet. I said a great friend of my sister, but nowadays, Paula and Rovena are more than just friends, they became part of my family. They spent three weeks with me there, long time to handle me, huh, girls? We were in this tiny room, we put a mattress on the floor, and we couldn't even open the closet at night because there was no space. And my bed was broken, so, one side was good to sleep, but the other? You would sleep and wake up with a strong back pain. Oh, and once there was a rat in the closet, that was something very traumatizing and all I can say is that we stayed 30 minutes on top of the kitchen table, screaming and terrified.

Two things I cannot deal with that make me like a scary child: cockroaches and rats. But rats are something you will see practically every day if you live in New York. Hopefully not in your bedroom and closet, only on the streets, and lots of them on the subway station. Just warning you. But besides the rats and all that jazz, we had so much fun. When classes started I couldn't give my new friends so much attention, but when I had a break, I would go meet them for dinner, or go to a bar. It was a true blast to have them with me.

There's this bar called Cafe Wha? In Greenwich Village. One of my favorite bars in NYC and a place that breathes music history. The club opened in 1959, and besides being a performance space for many legends in the sixties such as Bob Dylan, Jimi Hendrix, The Velvet Underground and Bruce Springsteen, it was also one of the epicenters of the Beat Movement, with regulars like Allen Ginsberg and Jack Kerouac, as well as comedians like Woody Allen, Richard Pryor and Bill Cosby, who also began their road in Cafe Wha? (Please go there, if you stop by New York). PS: Once we went there and there was this great cover band playing the song "Home" by Edward Sharpe and The Magnetic Zeros and Rovena fell in love with the singer. All she could talk about for the next few days was his beautiful voice, and how much she wanted to go back. We did, but there was another band playing.

We would go to Central Park at the weekends, walk around. We did a group on an app called "New York Folks" that we have until today, where we can chat, and even though all of us are in Brazil now, we still have it along with all the great memories of the time we spend together. Some people come to our lives in ways we don't expect and they become the best gifts in our lives. Paula and Rovena were people I could really count on, and still can.

Chapter 7

120 Madison Avenue

September 14th 2014 – I won't forget that day. It was the day that everything started for me at the American Academy of Dramatic Arts. I remember there were about a hundred of us sitting in one of the three theaters of the school and we were smiling at each other, talking to the ones sitting next to us. We were excited, jumpy to hear what the teachers and directors would say, what classes we would be in, who would be our classmates, etc. We heard some of the teachers talking, how much we would need to focus, take it seriously, every piece of work we do, every class, make a commitment and stick with it.

My first teacher was Chris Dolman, who's a sweet guy, but he knew how to push us further in his own way. I remember he asked us to make a list of what acting was for us, and here are some words and phrases we used: connection, vulnerability, awareness, trust, listening, being brave, being truthful, becoming the character, relating ourselves to the character, understanding what's going on in that moment, living in the moment, using our imagination, engaging, being present and focusing. Acting is all of that, it's what moves you, it's a point of view, it's perspective, it's a feeling and the meaning we give to it. Meaning is what makes acting, or any other thing, an ART. Utta Hagen describes all that with a simple sentence: "Acting is living truthfully under imaginary circumstances". To live truthfully means to do something, to act/react, when you have an obstacle.

The first assignment that Chris gave us was to observe our day and our response to the things in our daily lives. Even the smallest things are all real. We spend so much time on our cellphones nowadays, looking down at them, texting, not seeing our surroundings, not observing. To be an actor you must observe, you must observe the behavior of other people, see them entirely, you need to be aware of what's happening. I've learned from all those years studying in LA and NY that there's no end to learning how to act, we can always be better. There's no right or wrong in acting but simply being present, aware, focused, and listening to your partner in the scene. Because acting is not about you, but about the other person. If you are not truly listening, then you aren't present in the moment, living moment to moment, and if you are not doing that, you are not a real actor. "Life beats down and crushes the soul and art reminds you that you have one." - Stella Adler.

Another class – and how small but important it was – was when he asked us to bring an object, any object, but something meaningful to you. Listening to my fellow classmates talking about their objects was so touching and powerful. One of my classmates, who became a great friend of mine, talked about a pair of socks – yes, that's right, a pair of socks that a friend gave to her back in London and how they were connected to her mom and a funny game they used to play since she was a little girl, hiding things and surprising each other. Another classmate talked about a clock that reminded him of home, Canada. Cute, right? Simple little things.

I talked about a drawing that my little niece made for me before I left for the US. She drew three butterflies, representing my sister, herself and me, so I could always look at it and remember us, remember home and remember that we would always be together. It was a beautiful moment that we shared, and in that way, we became closer – not only classmates, but it was the beginning of a friendship. We opened ourselves up – acting is about that, and about being honest and truthful to ourselves and to others. We did an exercise where we would stay in pairs in front of each other and we would have to say the first thing that came into our minds. "You are smiling", "Your nose is big", whatever crossed your mind. You shouldn't think about it, just say it, and the other person would see something in you and reply to that. The words didn't seem to matter, but the reactions meant something. If the other person gets angry with something you say, don't think, respond to it. We want our most vulnerable side to come out of us. It was an exercise about our impulses and our unconsciousness.

I could go on and on just about Chris' classes and the first semester, but it was a two-year program, so I want to talk more about other teachers and what I learned from them. We also had one of the funniest teachers I've met, for Styles class I and II, but he could be harsh as well, which was good, not bad. We had Theater History classes with him and everyone was simply terrified of the exam because the graduation people said it was hard. Hard is good. Hard pushes us further, hard makes us challenge ourselves more. I always loved history, so that wasn't a problem for me. To be an actor, you also need to love reading, reading digital banners on the streets, newspapers, books, plays, articles, whatever you want, but you need to practice reading, exercising the brain like a muscle. You travel through time and space, you visit places by reading novels, plays, etc. Isn't that a gift? For me, definitely it is.

We learned about Greek theatre, Roman theatre, Transition and early Medieval theatre, High and late Medieval theatre, Commedia Dell'Arte & Renaissance (I must admit that was one of my favorites). English Elizabethan theatre, Spanish Golden Age theatre, French Baroque theatre, Restoration comedy, Neoclassical theatre, nineteenth century theatre – it goes on and on. We didn't have time to spend weeks and weeks on each one of them, but we had some basis and information about each one, and we were able to perform and create our own scenes, characters.

Commedia Dell'Arte, for example, utilized stock characters that were separated into three groups: the lovers, the masters, and the servants. The master was based usually on the stereotype of Pantalone, an elderly Venetian merchant; Dottore was Pantalone's friend or rival, while Capitano was once a lover character but evolved into a braggart who boasted of his exploits in love and war but was often hopelessly unskilled in both. The servant character was Arlecchino, ignorant yet cunning, but a very good dancer and acrobat. Todd gave us groups to create scenes for this type of theatre and period of time, and we used to spend hours trying to find a story and these characters. The results made all our classmates laugh. That is the biggest present we can give as actors, to touch others, whether it's with laughs or tears, or simply to see that they connected with something we did. That is enough for that day. For that performance.

We had on our first and second semester other classes such as Voice & Speech I, Mask, Movement, Musical Theatre, Dance Classes, and some I must be forgetting. I admire my school so much, and the years I spend there.

Voice & Speech classes. I had the best lady, the sweetest human being on earth, Becca McLarty. She was the sunlight entering our classroom, actually two suns, because she was pregnant with a beautiful little girl, who as I write is now two years old. Her voice was sweet and she gave this sense of peace, you know? But that doesn't mean she was easy on us. Our classes were fun, if everyone did their homework. We learned IPA (the International Phonetical Alphabet) – phonetic transcription, the study of the sounds of human speech. The pronunciation of the words varies depending on whether words are in stressed or weak positions in the sentences. We learned how to speak General American, we learned dialects, how to speak English with a German accent, a Japanese accent, a Spanish accent, or a British accent. Even with a Portuguese accent. Isn't that amazing? And we learned how to use the different dialects of the USA. The southern American accent, for example. This was a really difficult one for me because I had to learn not only for my own knowledge, but the last, final play we did was southern, so I had to really, really present myself and for others to believe I was from the southern states.

There are so many different dialects, but if you really learn phonetics, you are able to understand other languages and pronounce them, because you are not writing the words exactly, you are writing the sounds of the words. I was amazed. There's this exercise that she did with us which I still use nowadays when I need to express my feelings, put it all out. The beginning I can't remember, but the main words stood in my head: *"Look, when I say I want to see you, I mean now, I mean jump! Don't you ever tell me you don't have time to see me, ever!"* And with each one of us she made us repeat that again and again and again. When I did it, she was standing in front of me and said: "Laura, did she hear what you said? The person you are saying this to?" My answer was: "I don't think so". And she said: "Yeah, because she doesn't take you seriously. Say it from your heart, go, say it."

I kept saying it and man, even though it was just in my imagination, I saw that person in front of me and she did hear. I kept repeating those words. I was bursting into tears, then I repeated them again and again and she asked me to move my arms and my body as if I was throwing something away, and that changed everything. I felt in my guts, in my stomach, in all parts of my body, the emotion that was coming out and I screamed out those words. Then I cried again, and then I said it without any tears. Serious. Straightforward. She asked again: "Do you think the person you are talking to took you seriously now? "I said: "Yes, she did".

My teacher always said our body is our instrument, and it is. You can take so much from it. Our emotions are hidden inside, and sometimes, just the way you breathe. You need to breathe from your stomach, from your belly. Not your chest. The chest brings anxiety. It takes away the power of you as an actor.

We had so many exercises in just learning how to breathe, and I actually learned how to breathe. I can say that, even though it sounds weird. We learn that also in yoga and with our doctors. I learned from my Voice & Speech teacher, "Inhale and exhale. Breathe deep from your belly." I think I heard this phrase a thousand times during my time at the school. If you're anxious, nervous, afraid, if you just breathe, so much will be discovered.

Since I am talking about my lovely lady mentor, here's an image of a letter she wrote to help me get my 0-1 Visa, in case one day I tried – yes, I want to and I will.

Letter from Becca McLarty

September 20, 2016

Re. O-1 Petition for Laura Linn
To Whom It May Concern:

Please allow this letter to serve as my very strong recommendation of Laura Linn.

It was a great pleasure to have Laura in my Voice and Speech II class at the American Academy of Dramatic Arts (AADA). In the year that I worked with her I found Laura to be a hard-working, talented, and intelligent student who is eager to learn.

I am an actor and adjunct faculty member at such prestigious institutions as AADA, Marymount Manhattan College, and Pace University. I hold my M.F.A. in Acting from Brooklyn College and have performed extensively both regionally and in New York City. I greatly enjoy the relationship between performing on stage and screen and delving into the work of an actor in the classroom.

Laura was one of my most dedicated students. She is driven and sensitive and approaches the work with excitement and curiosity. Over the course of the academic year, Laura made great progress in gaining awareness of her breath, body, and vocal resonance in order to be fully present in her acting. She also made strides in the diction and dialect work. She is committed to her own process; determined to improve and grow even when the work challenges her academically and personally. She was also an enthusiastic supporter of her classmates. Her warm and attentive nature greatly contributed to the strength of the ensemble in our classroom.

Since graduating, Laura has continued to push herself. She looks not only to improve her own craft, but passionately strives to make a contribution to her artistic community and our society at large. I look forward to seeing all that Laura accomplishes. She is true artist and is truly deserving of the classification of Foreign Citizen of Extraordinary Ability in the Arts. Please reach out to me if you have any questions. I can be reached at 717.682.1910.

Sincerely,

Becca L. McLarty

Not much else needs to be said if you read the letter above. But those people who saw my effort and my true self, and helped me discover it even more, changed my life and made me become a better person.

I couldn't forget to talk about our king. The king of Voice & Speech in the United States of America, for me and so many other students there, was Jim DeMonic with his funny stories. He always had a story to tell, always with patience and a kind smile, kindness was his last name. And knowledge was his first name. Every question I had about voice & speech, about phonetic transcription, he was the guy I looked for, in his tiny little office on the fourth floor next to the bathroom. Jim was there 24/7, available. Tired, exhausted, but always there for us. I've never seen someone like what they do as a profession so much as he does.

Here's another letter, from Chris Dolman, my first acting teacher at AADA, who wanted to help me and saw some potential in me. (see over)

LAURA LINN

April 7, 2016

To Whom It May Concern:

I am writing in strong support of Laura Linn and her application for O-1 status. Ms. Linn was a student in my 2014 1ˢᵗ Year Acting and 2015 Acting Is A Business classes at the American Academy of Dramatic Arts (AADA), America's first acting conservatory. I have also observed her work in studio and onstage at the conservatory. I have worked for over 20 years in the theatre, film and television industries as an actor, director, producer and teacher and feel I am qualified to accurately evaluate Ms. Linn's unique artistic gifts and prospects for success in the United States.

Laura, a 2016 graduate of AADA, has proven herself to be an extraordinary theatre artist whose work suggests that she will make a strong contribution to the arts in this country. She has shown significant growth in her performance skills along with a strong desire to learn how the course material is applicable in her career development. She proved herself to be a reliable and active participant when working with others on group projects. She also has revealed proven leadership qualities as other students looked to her for guidance. Staff, faculty and theatrical directors believe in her talent and have consistently given her responsibilities comiserate with artists of the highest caliber who have matriculated at school over the years.

In addition to completing her two year training, Laura has already begun to make progress in her professional career, having been offered roles in two short film by Los Angless based screenwriter Rafael Stiborski and she is currently in meetings with feature film producer Rose Ganguzza. In the ultra- competitive acting industry it is significant that Laura has already begun to work in her profession. As an Artistic Associate at a pre-eminent regional theatre who regularly hires actors, it is rare to see an artist as determined to succeed as Laura.

I would be remiss if I did not also say that Laura has shown herself to be thoughtful, generous of spirit and personable with a good sense of humor. I recommend her without hesitation. If you have any questions please call me at 212-769-9613.

Sincerely,

Chris Dolman
Acting Instructor, American Academy of Dramatic Arts
Artistic Associate, Cape May Stage

Grandpa and me at The Botanical Garden

Little adventurer since 1991

"Hello, it's me. I was wondering if after all these years you'd like to meet"

Guess I was tired of the bangs, so I did it myself.

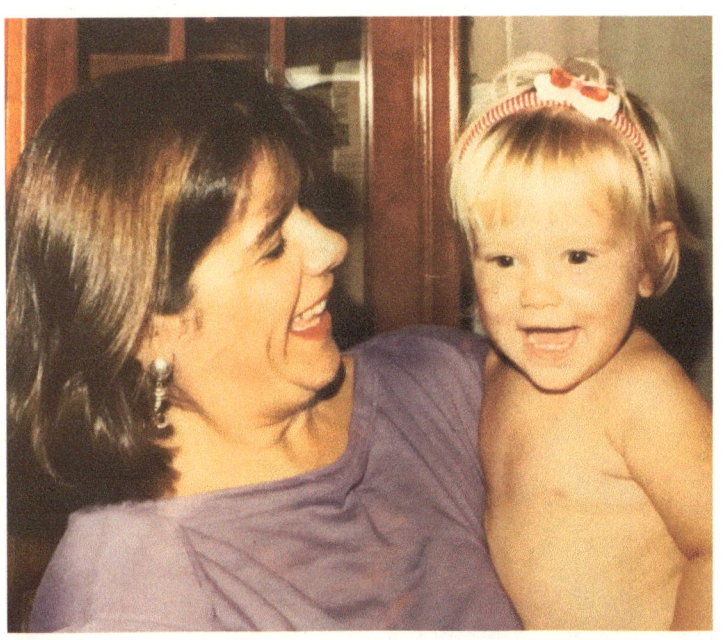

I love you to the moon and back.

Mini me with mom and dad

Paulie and Rovi in Brooklyn

My soul sister Cintia
& baby Lana

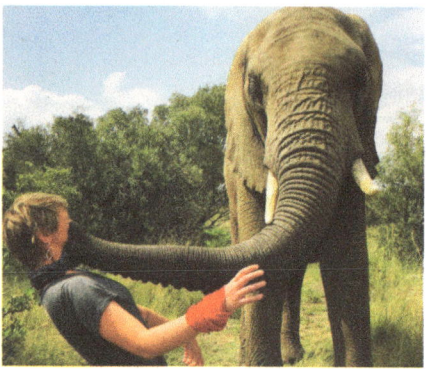

The most passionate kiss of my life!
Chishuru and me in South Africa

London calling

Double love, double happiness. Quim & Tom

"My girls, I'm talking about my girls."

Real NYC winter

No pain, no gain - movie preparation

More than 10 years of friendship, and many stories to tell

The women of my life - my mom and sister

Unconditional love

Me and Tarzan, my partner in crime and in scene!

Best buddy!

Me and the Goddess, Cate Blanchett on her Broadway debut

Why so serious?! My princess

A transformation

Photoshoot

"I could hold you in my arms, I could hold you forever"

"California here we come, right back where we started from"

The greatest joy - graduation play at the American Academy
of Dramatic Arts

Where's Waldo? Majestic Theatre, NYC - 2016. Actors in action!

My tiny big wolf, Noah

Ready – set – go!

Wherever you are, exploring the world, my heart
is with you and I miss you.

Ommmmmmmm...

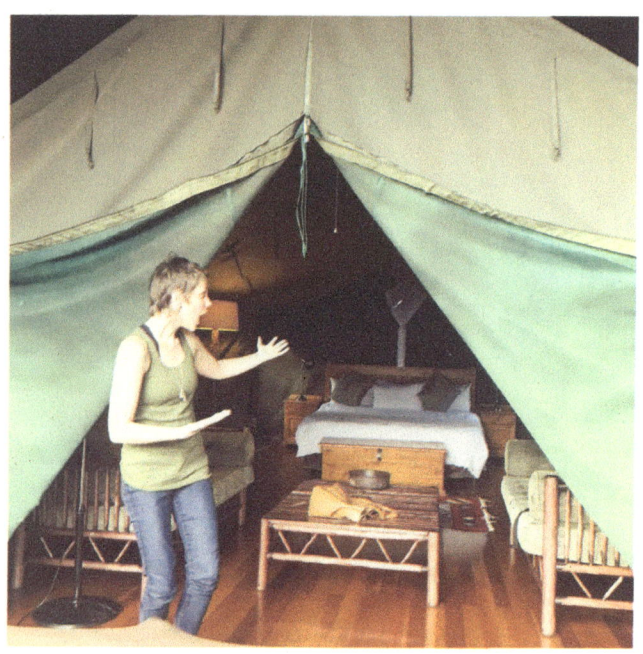

Is this real? A cabin in the woods (or is it a tent?)

We can be a thousand miles away, but the love remains the same.

My South African family - How the movie journey began

The Furnace

And... ACTION! I'm the luckiest person to work with this genius writer & director, Darrell Roodt.

It can't get cuter than this. Into the wild.

Hello there, little guy!

Enjoying the beach at Camps Bay, South Africa

The Campos siblings

Thanks for being in my life!

My Pisces girl and Juliet

Laugh until your belly hurts

NGO for Social Inclusion through music and dance that my aunt Maria Teresa Campos built. "Sol Maior" - biggest sun. Seeing these happy faces is the true blessing.

My world traveler, so much love for you!

Together forever. Family, the greatest gift of all

Quick family nap in the High Line, New York

One of my favorite actresses from our home, Brazil, Dani Suzuki

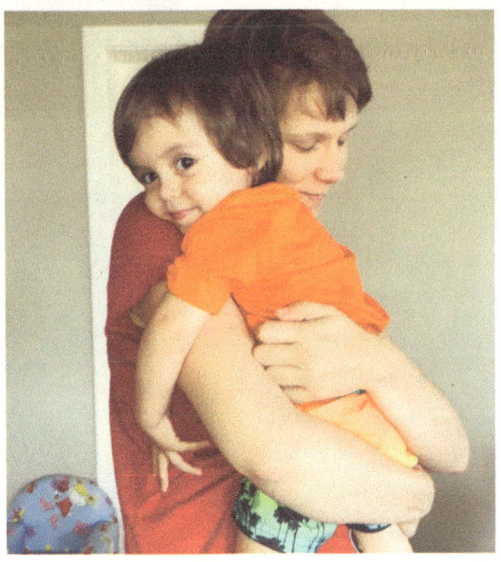

The best hug in the world

Dad and Geo

My princess

"Ohana means family, family means nobody gets left behind or forgotten."

My name is Flavia Amon and I am a friend of the actress Laura Linn.
She recently graduated from the prestigious American Academy of Dramatic Arts in New York where she completed the 2 year Conservatory Program. At AADA she had the opportunity to work with the actor Frank Langella and recently showcased her talents at the Actors Artistry in Los Angeles.

I'm VP of Creative Advertising at Fox Searchlight Pictures.
Since 2000 I've collaborated on the creative advertising campaigns of over 100 films including
114 Oscar nominations and 31 Wins.

I've known Laura for more than 4 years and I can say that she i a true artist, very passionate, hard working, thoughtful, sensitive and a person of great integrity.

She is currently looking for representation, someone that will partner with her and help guide her career.
I am here to present myself as a referral and recommend her without hesitation.

I appreciate your consideration and time.

Kindly,

Flavia Amon
12/14/16

And a letter from Flavia Amon, the greatest producer and most determined woman I ever met. She knew my dad because he helped her with her wedding in the north of Brazil, years and years ago, and the first time I went to LA, she welcomed me in the Fox Studios. I remember the first time I went there – my eyes were shining, smiling ear from ear, and people like Danny

Boyle (one of the greatest directors of all time, in my opinion) were passing by and saying hi. We used to have quick lunches together, because the work demands were huge, but she always believed in me and supported me as well. I hope, one day, maybe with this book, I will show how thankful I am for these "little" things, things that mean the world to you, and in baby steps you can achieve your goals, with good people by your side. And these friends, teachers, mentors helped me along all the way.

The letter from Darrell Roodt, director of The Furnace. (Opposite)

October 31st 2017

Re. O-1 Petition for Laura Linn
To Whom It May Concern:

I am writing this recommendation letter in strong support for Ms. Laura Linn and her application for the 0-1 status.

My name is Darrell James Roodt, I am a South African director and screenwriter. I've been working in the film industry for more than 30 years. I met Laura Linn through Andre Frauenstein, a producer from Phoenix Films in South Africa. I've worked in many movies with Andre and his production company. Reine Swart, a South African actress that studied with her in 2010 at the New York Film Academy recommended her to Andre Frauenstein saying that she is a great actress.

I have directed many actors including Whoopi Goldberg in "Sarafina", Patrick Swayze in my movie "Father Hood", James Earl Jones in "Cry, the Beloved Country, among other. My film "Yesterday" was nominated for the Academy Award for Best Foreign Language Movie and also the Independent Spirit Awards for Best Foreign Film in 2005.

Laura and I are working on a project together, a feature movie called "The Furnace" that is in pre-production right now. Laura will play an important role in the movie: Rafaela. Laura has shown so much effort and talent. She has proven herself to be an amazing artist, preparing for her character in the movie. She dedicated her whole time to immerse herself into the story. Making a huge transformation physically and emotionally for it. I had the pleasure of meeting her personally in South Africa and talk to her about the movie. I look forward to direct her in this project.

Laura is without doubt an extraordinary actress. She was invited to study and graduated in one of the best schools in the USA, The American Academy of Dramatic Arts (AADA) in New York City. She worked in many short films and commercials, back in country in Brazil and also while she was on her work permit in New York, after graduating. She showed an incredible work ethic. She is a true artist and the world should give a chance to see her talent and for her to pursue her career in the USA. I can say with no doubt that Laura Linn deserves the O-1 Visa and I recommend her without hesitation. Her talent and artistic contribution to the United States of America would be quite significant. I believe that she is completely qualified and worthy of receiving the classification of Foreign Citizen of Extraordinary Ability in the Arts. If you have any questions, please contact me at +27 (82) 900-9418 (South African Number).

Sincerely,

Darrell James Roodt
Oscar Nominated Director and Screenwriter

Chapter 8

Making like Fire

Back to AADA and Movement classes. For someone who wasn't such a big fan of exercises, that was tough, man. I had Angela Nahigian – "yesssss, breeeeathe from youuuur bellyyyyyy", she used to talk like that, yes and it was inspiring – and also I had Sheila Bandyopadhyay as a teacher; Angela in the first semester and Sheila in second or third semester, but Sheila was also my Mask teacher. Angela used to give us this funny look, to intimidate us. We went crazy in those classes, we did yoga, but we also moved around, played at being animals – we had to go to the zoo to observe an animal and then for three or four minutes just be that animal 100%.

I guess the toughest exercise was doing the back bridge with our body and not only have to stay there with the bridge but actually move with it from one side of the classroom to the other, with no sense of direction at all, since our heads were upside down. Oh, and we always did the downward dog, every 20 minutes of yoga when classes started. We imitated snakes, dolphins, reptiles, whales, and other animals I didn't know, didn't even know what they were or how they moved. We had to incorporate colors – that's right. How does the color yellow move? Think about it. Think about the emotions that yellow gives to you when you look at it. How does the color red move and feel? Both Angela and Sheila worked on that with us.

We did monologues just with our body expressions. We once made a tree with our body, from being a tiny small seed until it starts growing and growing and making the seasons: spring, summer, fall and winter. The leaves falling. Everything. Our teachers recommended us to write a diary every single day, about the classes, what we thought that day, etc. I have kept my diaries in a secret place, like gold. If I were to describe every class here, I would have a 200-page book just about the classes, but my intention is to share some special, significant moments, chosen with love, of my life and experiences living abroad.

I also have to talk about the Mask classes, because they were life changing. We used neutral masks and we had to perform, create scenes and project ourselves with our bodies, since with the mask on, there was no facial expression. It was all about movement, discovering the characters through our actions, body movements. We had to learn how to be fire, water, earth and air. I asked myself as soon as Sheila told us that: How am I going to be fire? Well, explore your body and you will find the fire, the water, the air, the earth. Thank you, Sheila and Angela, for all you've taught me. Your strength, knowledge and sensibility made me a better actor.

Shakespeare's characters were based on that. The four humors were blood, yellow bile, black bile (or melancholy) and phlegm. Each was linked with one of the four elements of earth, water, air and fire; the four qualities of cold, hot, moist and dry, based on the four bodily humors inherited from the ancient Greek philosophers Aristotle, Hippocrates and Galen. These physical qualities were said to determine the behavior of all created things, including the human body. The humors affect your whole being, from your health and feelings to your looks and actions. If blood dominates, you will have a sanguine temperament; yellow bile makes you choleric; black bile melancholic; and phlegm leads you to being phlegmatic.

In *Henry IV*, parts one and two, there are four main characters, one of each temperament, and they all have roughly the same number of lines. King Henry VI was melancholic, Prince Hal was sanguine, Sir Harry Hotspur choleric and the knight Sir John Falstaff is phlegmatic. How incredible is that? I learned how to respect and love Shakespeare even more. I read *Othello* again, *As You Like It, Comedy of Errors, Merchant of Venice, Midsummer Night's Dream, The Tempest, Twelfth Night, Winter's Tale*, the classics *Macbeth, Romeo and Juliet, King Lear*, and I read them two or three times each until I could finally understand what they were about. For me, Shakespeare was able to explore all the emotions of us human beings in his plays. The characters are complex simulations of thinking and feeling in action. He captured fundamental concepts about how our minds work. Macbeth, for example, brings ambition, conflict, corruption, order and disorder, guilt, sin and retribution, power, good and bad, and many more. Each play brings out different emotions and different sides of us. Shakespeare explores them dramatically through his characters, and these characters define the play. Each play explores its own issues. Many people might dislike Shakespeare, and that's OK. I just share my thoughts about him and how much I learned from this.

Barbara Rubin was my teacher for the Shakespeare class. She was my hero in that school. She made us dive into Shakespeare, learn how to read it, because Shakespeare's language isn't easy, specially if English is not your first language. We had to learn the iambic pentameter pattern, which is a metrical line in traditional English poetry and verse drama. The term shows the rhythm of the words in each line, measured in groups of syllables called "feet". "Iambic" refers to an unstressed syllable followed by a stressed syllable, and "pentameter" indicates that a line has five of these "feet". Shakespeare's dramatic verse is often referred to as "blank verse", because it doesn't rhyme, except often in the last two lines of a speech. The iambic pentameter pattern was used commonly in English poetry from Chaucer onwards, and here's a simple example of a Iambic Pentameter from Romeo and Juliet play. The (ˇ) is for unstressed syllables and (/) for the stressed ones:

ˇ　　/　　ˇ　　/　　ˇ　　/　ˇ　/　ˇ　　/

But soft, what light through yonder window breaks? (2.2.2)

And that gives a rhythm: 'de-DUM, de-DUM, de-DUM, de-DUM, de-DUM'. The rhythmic unit of Shakespeare's blank verse contains two syllables, with the stress falling on the second syllable ('de-DUM'). We went play by play, pieces of it, studying the iambic pentameter and taking home some exercises to be done. Every monologue we did in class, we had to do the iambic pentameter and also a translation, translating every word of Shakespeare's piece. For example, with the line above, we needed to find synonyms for soft, light, through, window, breaks — every single word, so we could fully understand. And then we would do our personal translation, what those words meant for us, who were we speaking to.

I did the famous scene where Juliet is on the balcony as she talks to Romeo. She starts talking of her embarrassment at being overheard, and goes on to make a declaration, fearlessness made possible by dark wild blue yonder, and that speech made me fall in love with her and this story.

Thou know'st the mask of night is on my face,
Else would a maiden blush bepaint my cheek
For that which thou hast heard me speak tonight.
Fain would I dwell on form. Fain, fain deny
What I have spoke. But farewell compliment!
Dost thou love me? I know thou wilt say "ay,"
And I will take thy word. Yet if thou swear'st
Thou mayst prove false. At lovers' perjuries,
They say, Jove laughs. O gentle Romeo,

If thou dost love, pronounce it faithfully.
Or if thou think'st I am too quickly won,
I'll frown and be perverse and say thee nay,
So thou wilt woo. But else, not for the world.
In truth, fair Montague, I am too fond,
And therefore thou mayst think my 'havior light.
But trust me, gentleman, I'll prove more true
Than those that have more coying to be strange.
I should have been more strange, I must confess,
But that thou overheard'st, ere I was 'ware,
My true love's passion. Therefore pardon me,
And not impute this yielding to light love,
Which the dark night hath so discovered.

Juliet opens herself, shows her vulnerable side, but with courage. She takes the chance and declares her love for Romeo, with her insecurity and fears too. If you take your time to understand each word of this speech, it will touch your soul so deeply that you will never forget. It was like that for me. I imagined my Romeo and spoke with all my heart.

The nine questions you need to ask yourself as an actor

As Utta Hagen wrote in her book *Respect for Acting*, there are nine questions you need to ask yourself to really connect to your character:

1. WHO AM I?
(All the details about your character including name, age, address, relatives, likes, dislikes, hobbies, career, description of physical traits, opinions, beliefs, religion, education, origins, enemies, loved ones, sociological influences, etc.)

2. WHAT TIME IS IT?
(Century, season, year, day, minute, significance of time)

3. WHERE AM I?
(Country, city, neighborhood, home, room, area of room)

4. WHAT SURROUNDS ME?
(Animate and inanimate objects – complete details of environment)

5. WHAT ARE THE GIVEN CIRCUMSTANCES?
(Past, present, future and all of the events)

6. WHAT IS MY RELATIONSHIP?
(Relation to total events, other characters, and to things)

7. WHAT DO I WANT?
(Character's need. The immediate and main objective)

8. WHAT IS IN MY WAY?
(The obstacles which prevent the character from getting his/her need)

9. WHAT DO I DO TO GET WHAT I WANT?
(The action: physical and verbal, also-action verbs)

These are the questions we must ask ourselves and explore and define in order to act truthfully.

I learned so many things in those two years. I learned to have more confidence, self-esteem. After answering these questions for every character I did, I let go. As one of my teachers said: when you enter an audition room, if you did your homework well, your research, just throw everything out of the window and live that moment. Take the focus out of yourself, and put into what is happening right now, the person you are talking to, just go with the feeling.

Burke was another of my acting teachers, he had his own way of teaching, and it was so different and nice. After each scene we did, he would ask: How do you feel? How was it for you? He allowed us to feel more relaxed to share, and he has definitely taught me so much about myself and acting. I am so thankful to him. Susan Pilar is another inspiration to me, as a teacher and as an actor. I didn't have the opportunity to actually work in class with her but every time we saw each other, and talked, and all her encouragement and advices made me stronger.

I'm sharing some of my exam progress reports, one from Jim Demonic, my Voice & Speech teacher, and one from Burke Pearson, my acting teacher. I'll keep reading this when I feel I need to, when I want to remember those times, and trust myself more. And you out there who is an actor, should always remind as well of the good moments, the good feedbacks you had that will help you to keep on going.

Jim wrote:

"Laura has demonstrated a positive attitude throughout the rehearsal process. She is open to criticism, and readily attempt to assimilate notes. She takes directions well and properly. She has demonstrated an ability to work simply and honestly, moment-to-moment. She has good emotional availability and imagination."

Burke wrote to me:

"Excellent student, intelligent, devoted, mature for her age, but shows tension, seems to be working under pressure sometimes. She demonstrates strong studentship elements, attentive in class, exercises are well prepared, written assignments detailed and responsive. Has strong sense of belief and is exceptionally present in the work, with point of view

*and strong pursuit of objectives that move her through a wide range of emotional response. Willing to risk and let the exercises reveal her. She's a good listener. Relationships and place work coming into focus. **Needs to relax and find confidence in herself, know she has a right to be here, know that she's earned it.** Nothing to be gained from putting pressure on yourself. You have excellent instincts for this work, both for power and vulnerability... Play truthfully off behavior of your partner and you'll discover the joy of spontaneity, and letting the scene take you where it wants to go."*

I emphasized the phrase 'needs to relax' because that's something all of my teachers used to say to me. And it meant the world to me to read that over and over again: "Know I have the right to be here, that I earned it." Some people think that actors have so much confidence to do this kind of work, because we need to be transparent, show our feelings, but most of us aren't that confident, we are insecure, and that's part of it. But we keep on learning to believe in ourselves more and more, with practice, with exercises, listening, and it's a work in progress. Even famous actors say how insecure they feel when doing a movie, or a specific scene. It's part of being human. We cannot let the insecurity and fears take over, in fact we must use them as a tool in our craft.

Maybe you are getting tired of reading about acting, if you are not an actor, but when I talk about my love and passion for acting and my experiences I am also talking about life, about feelings, about stories. Stories that everyone can relate to. From classic plays to contemporary plays, we are talking about people. Emotions. So I hope you are enjoying this journey with me as I write my memories.

After the first year was done, we all had a break and I went home, back to Brazil, not knowing if I was going to be called back for the second year. But I was happy to be back in my city and seeing my friends again, my family, spend time with my niece. But home is where your heart is and mine was still in the USA – my mission there wasn't finished, it was just beginning. So, even without expectations to be back for the second year, I knew I had to go back.

One month after I was back home, I received the email I was waiting for saying: "You are invited to join the second year at our school". I recall the enthusiasm, I recall myself jumping in my mom's arms and saying: "I was accepted, mom, I am going back to NY!" I cried tears of happiness, tears of joy. Many students weren't invited for the second year and to know I was one of the ones who were made that phrase that Burke told me, to believe in myself, trust that I deserved to be there, echo in my mind. So I went back, to continue my mission, to complete my degree.

The second year was even more challenging, and the classes even more exciting. We had fencing class, stage combat, theatre dance, and at the end of each semester, we did a play. The last semester of the second year had less classes, because we were working on two final plays.

My teacher for Acting during second year was a guy called Zenon Kruszelnicki. This guy changed me. And every person that was in my classroom had a reason to be there, being taught by Zenon. We didn't know why, but the teachers were so attentive and concerned with our growth that everything was done precisely and for a certain motive. Oh, Zenon – our Polish acting teacher and director.

Every teacher had a different way to teach us. And Zenon, he was just a *bomb*, ready to explore at any minute. I don't even know how to describe him. He was fire. He was so passionate. He provoked us, he made us feel real, alive. He used to start classes with a lot of physical exercises, and I mean a lot, for real. Like jumping 200 times, nonstop, touching your knees in your chest, until we dropped on the floor, exhausted. Once I said to him when I simply fell on the floor and couldn't breathe: "I can't do it anymore, Zenon". He said: "Never talk to me again that way. Now get up and keep doing it." Yes, he was harsh on us, but that was because he knew we could do it, he knew we were stronger than we imagined. A great mentor, teacher and person.

We did a lot of sense memory work, training our senses to respond on the stage as they do in life, concentrating on the stimuli associated with a sensory experience. If the actor really believes that what he is doing is real, then the audience will also believe it is real. It was a key to unlock the door of imagined reality.

One of the many exercises we did started by lying on the floor. Zenon would guide us through his voice, explaining what was happening, preparing us. Then he said: "There's a guy with a gun outside our building and he is entering right now, open your eyes." We opened them. He said, "now he is walking towards our classroom, you can hear the screams outside, and he's getting closer and closer to our door. We hear the shot of a gun. And more screams." We were all in panic, it felt so real, as if the guy really was there. "Everyone stay quiet and hide". We all tried to find a place to hide. I couldn't even breathe, I was behind a chair, holding my friend's hand, Sequoia, and saying to myself "Please, please, don't enter, don't enter, please God, help us". And later, Zenon said: "Done". So we could get out of the exercise, but it took me 20 minutes to be able to cool down, to fall back into reality and realize it was just an exercise. But that just shows how far our imagination can go.

Another example is pretending to be in Antarctica, freezing. It's hot in the classroom, but we need to create the feeling of being cold. You can *play* cold, shivering, wrapping your arms around yourself, but you want to create the reality, not play. So you need to use sensorial recall, and ask yourself how the cold affects you. It affects your ears, your nose. Your fingers get stiff, your lips get numb, it's hard to move. Those are things that will make it real, for yourself and the audience. The five senses need to be explored. Closing your eyes and remembering the *taste* of your favorite food, but really trying to taste and recall how it was; *hearing* your mom's voice calling you when you were little; *touching* a silk sheet, how it feels; *smelling* your favorite perfume; the *sight* of your favorite place on earth, the beach, the ocean, the forest. The sense memory exercise helps to find the reality of these situations.

Zenon did a lot of that with us, and always gave us meaningful scenes that we could connect to it. He gave me one of my biggest challenges as an actor, a play called *Venus in Fur* by David Ives. This play-within-the play is an adaptation of an 1870 novel called *Venus in Furs* by Leopold von Sacher-Masoch, Austrian author – the term "masochism" was actually inspired by him. I played Vanda Jordan, a vulgar woman who tries to persuade the director, Novacheck, let her audition for the part of Wanda. A lot happens during that play, and it was a big challenge because not only did I, Laura Linn, play Vanda Jordan, but I was also playing Vanda Jordan doing an audition for another character, Wanda Von Dunayev. Both characters become caught up in the characters they are reading. It's a play about dominance. The power is reversed from Novachek to Vanda, and that also occurs in the novel by Leopold. I actually had to go to a sex shop in New York and buy a sexy outfit, a whip, handcuffs, gloves and high heels to do this character. And at the time, for me, Laura, that was the extreme opposite of who I was or who I was used to playing as an actor. Usually I played characters who were kind of romantic, easy going.

Zenon went to the opposite side of that, he wanted to see if I had the sexy, eager Laura inside of me. He pushed me. He used to stop the scene over and over again and say: "Laura, hit him harder! Laura, I'm not seeing a sexy woman in front of me. Laura, you don't even know how to walk with high heels?" And all of that he was saying not only to me but in front of all the classroom. Some of my friends/classmates asked me, how were you able to handle it? I simply did. I was crying inside, but I was so angry at the same time that it actually helped me. At the end of the scene, I was crying, and he said: "Sit down, write how you are feeling and stop crying. This is not professional". That day changed me entirely. I was furious inside, and sad, and feeling terrible. But at the end of the class I went up to him and said, "Thank you, Zenon". And he said, "You are welcome, Laura. I had to do this, because I know that you have this other side of you, you are just too afraid to reveal it. You are capable of so much more, if you just trust yourself and not worry what other people will think".

Nowadays, I call him Z or reference him as like the teacher from the movie *Whiplash*. If you have seen this movie, just saying that Z was like that teacher is enough to understand his way of pushing us. But for the best, always.

That was my big lesson, and I still carry it with me. Every single teacher and director I had in that school made me a better actor and a stronger person. They didn't take away my humility, they gave me even more. Actors have to be humble. But they gave me so much. Knowledge. Confidence. Strength. Kindness. Empathy. Love. Focus. Respect. Courage. And the list goes on. Being thankful and grateful aren't enough to describe what I feel for all of those who lived those moments with me, all my classmates, such talented people, all my teachers, all my directors. All I can say is that every lesson I will take with me everywhere I go.

Theatre vs. film

One of my favorite books about acting is called *Acting in Film* by the English actor Michael Caine. In it he talks a lot about his experiences as an actor, the differences between acting in theatre and acting in movies. If you are a stage actor it doesn't mean you are better or worse than a movie actor. It's all about being truthful and living in the moment. But there are differences. If you are on stage, you feel the energy of the audience, even if you don't look at them, can't see them, you know they are there, there's this vibration that makes your heart beat fast – you are live, there's no pause button or "cut" from the director. When you start a play, you start it and you finish it, you go until the end of it. You live the story, you live the character for those 60 minutes or 80 minutes or 120 minutes. You tell the story in an order, how it was written. Nevertheless, it's worth it. But it's hard to be fully connected and present moment to moment for all that time, nonstop. And you have to speak louder – not screaming, but that's why it's so important to learn how to project your voice and still be genuine. You don't have to be big. You just have to project it so people can hear you, but it has to come from inside.

When you finish the play and hear the applause, when you come out of the stage and someone comes to you and says, "I was so moved by it, I remembered my son when you did that scene where you were talking to him", that's our prize as actors. To go home knowing that maybe not everyone in the audience loved it, but some did, some people will also go home thinking about it, remembering it. And in theatre there are usually no "records" of it, except some pictures. I love it. I love it so much, it's just that moment, you, your acting partners, the crew who are working on it, the director, the stage manager, and those 100, 200, 300, 1,000 people on the theatre living with you that story.

That's one of the big differences about acting in movies: You recorded it. In a movie set, you might start with scene 20 at the beginning of day one, and the next day you might be doing scene 35, then scene 1. There's no order. Some people say: Yeah, but you can always do it again, cut it, until you "get there", where you wanted to, where the director wanted you to be. You can see from this side, but you can also see the other side of it.

Imagine having to do a scene where you lose your daughter, you receive a call saying she's dead. Now imagine doing this scene 30 times. Having the emotions inside of you to repeat that, to be surprised with the information you just received and the state you find yourself in, shocked, paralyzed, sad, speechless. And maybe on take 1 or 4 you found your truthful moment, but because of the lighting or the sound, it didn't work. So you have to do it again, and even being surrounded by 40, 50 people, you have to focus on you and convey that emotion with a look, sometimes, when the camera is shooting a close up of just your eyes.

So there's no better or worse between acting in theatre and movies, just differences. However, in both cases you must be honest, connected and listening. People forget one of the most important parts of acting: listening. Truly listening to what's being said to you. And then respond to that.

So as you see, acting isn't easy work. It's going to challenge you in many ways, as long as you challenge yourself to grow, to go beyond your comfort zone, to take risks and not be safe in terms of protecting yourself from taking on new experiences. This work will make great demands on you. At times you will feel excited, frustrated, hate the monotony, hate yourself, hate your partners sometimes, love them other times. But ask why you are feeling that way and simply accept and honor those feelings – keep working, keep doing the exercises.

Don't let your feelings day to day get in the way of doing the exercises. The work you do outside of class is as important, or more, than the work you do in class. Have your feelings. Honor them and keep working. Be honest to yourself. Are you ready to be more expressive, more spontaneous, more willing to fight for what is true? Are you ready to become more fully authentic and alive in your acting? If so, then this is the approach to acting for you. The work will lead you to acting with deeper personal meaning and a wonderful simplicity, if you let it. You must be ruthlessly honest with yourself, don't let yourself take the easy way out or to slack off. Together we can build an acting exercise that ultimately contains all the dramatic elements. As you practice these exercises your acting skills will grow and strengthen. The key is to do it consistently. With hard work and time, your technique will grow. You will only get out of this as much as you put into it, it's that simple. "An actor has to burn inside with an outer ease" – Michael Chekhov.

I won't take much longer on the two-year program. I guess I talked enough for this book, but a little part I do need to talk about is the graduation, April 11th 2016. It was such a special day, sunny and beautiful outside. Our class was the 131st Graduation Class and the Ceremony was at the Majestic Theatre, on West 44th Street. Fanciest night of my life, and one of the happiest. It completed my journey at the school, mission accomplished. But the journey of acting and learning was just starting.

During these 2 years at The Academy I had

incredible classmates and made true friendships. People from all over the world, different countries, different cultures, different states, but inside that building and classes we created a family, we shared moments, feelings that we will never forget. I had the honor to work with some pretty damn talented actors, and believe me, you will hear these names: Taylor Peer, Eni Tóth Bagi, Sarah Gardner, Unnur Eggertsdóttir, Julia Bostrom, Alana DeGregorio, Sabrina Monique, Megan Schadler, Sam Kate Green, Aisha N'Jaye, Christelle Belinga, Francesca Dolan, Tatiana Gurevich, Brett Michael Bullard, Sequoia Davis, Michaela DeBruhl, Darby Alice Bixler, Ekaterina Golovina, Gaia Passaler, Vince Vaughan, Siri Nerland, Clarie D'Angelo, Hannah Taylor, Kimisha Edwards, Ryan Murnane, Samantha Jo, Larry Lange, Maddy Rotarius, Monica Gronchi, Sen Enver, Nick Newling, Isabella Barzuna, Alexander Hodge, Ariana Wellmoney, Liam Amstrong, Tanya Palkaninec, Katie Puschel, Eliza Shea, Connor Delves, Ellie Rhodes, Ryan Attie, Jeffrey Alkins, Dan Kauss, Celia Rocha, Jada Bennett. These people gave their best, work their asses off and we all grew as actors so much, with the help of our teachers and helping one another. Now we are out there, searching for our dreams and I hope that each one of these amazing actors, find their path, because they have what it takes, even if some of them decide not to pursue this career, I am sure that we all learned so much between those walls, classrooms, inside and out the stage. And these lessons we will take with us whatever we go.

There are many acting techniques: the Stanislavski System, the Lee Strasberg Method, Stella Adler, the Meisner Technique, Uta Hagen - I mentioned some of her techniques before in the book - and others, and what all these techniques have in common is that they all seek for true connection and to have an intention as a character. You need to have an OBJECTIVE, know what your main objective is in the script, and then be able to break down the scenes, find the objectives in each scene that lead to your overall objective, and that objective has to be strong.

Chapter 9

New York Winter

Now let's take a break from acting, and talk about New York and how my routine was, how I survived in the city.

Well, as you might have heard, or if you have visited NYC, it's not a cheap city. It is actually one of the most expensive places in the USA to live in. And survive. And feed yourself. And it gets so cold in the winter that you just want to stay in bed the entire day watching Netflix in your PJs. That happened to me practically the entire two winters I spent in NYC. It kind of makes you depressed. I know, I know, you must be thinking, how can I complain if I am living in a city that so many people would give a finger to live in, or just to visit? Or maybe not. I don't know you. Maybe I will, someday. Who knows? Life is full of surprises. And if you got as far as this page, I just want to say thank you and that I hope you can relate to some of these stories or laugh, or cry, or whatever you want.

Back to the cold. As I talked to many friends of mine who were living in NYC, or were born there, and "used to" the cold, nah, that's kind of bull****. In 2014, the news was everywhere: Record-Breaking Cold Hits New York City.

"Temperatures hit historic lows overnight in New York City, according to the National Weather Service. A reading of 4 degrees was recorded in Central Park and at La Guardia Airport earlier Tuesday morning, breaking the record of 6 degrees set for Jan. 7 that dated back to 1896, according to a spokeswoman. This is the coldest temperature recorded in Central Park in almost a decade; the mercury last dropped this low on Jan. 14, 2004, when it bottomed out at 2 degrees, the NWS said."

That 4°F is equivalent to -15°C, and although that was the real temperature it felt like -30°C. I know a lot of us say we Sagittarius people exaggerate, but I am saying the truth. That's how I felt. I would go out to school with a stockpile of base layers of clothes, plus a huge coat, a giant scarf to protect my neck, a thin down puffer for layering, a good pair of gloves, boots to battle slush puddles, earmuffs for the hat-hair phobic, sweaters, socks and tights for layering. Yeah, you need all that for your 30-minute transportation and then you take everything out when you get inside a coffee place, a bar, the school, the theatre, because the heating works in the USA. So it's this tiring thing, put 100 layers of clothes on then take it all off, then put it all again. Not complaining, just saying how it is, if you don't want to get sick and freeze to death. Just saying.

But OK. If you are able to survive the cold, the seasons in New York, autumn and spring are just incredible, and so beautiful. Every autumn, NYC's thousands of trees burst into a riot of vibrant colors. It's just beautiful to see the fall foliage in many gardens and the New York City parks. In Central Park, I used to spend hours and hours just sitting by a tree, reading a play, or writing in my diary. I didn't need anything else. Feeling the leaves crunch beneath my feet. And so much happens in the city during the autumn, the Thanksgiving Day Parade, the NYC Marathon, the Village Halloween Parade and much more.

The spring brings warmer temperatures, and you can appreciate the cherry blossoms in the botanic gardens, take long walks in Prospect Park or Central Park or anywhere you want, because it's getting warmer and the temperature is so nice. Go and have a long, delicious brunch at Sarabeth's, one of my favorite places for brunch. Ask for the Eggs Benedict there, if you go, please. You deserve it (if you like eggs, if not, ask for the pancakes, they are delicious, too). They have it in Tribeca and other places, but the one close to Central Park is my favorite. Oh, so many coffee shops and nice restaurants to go. If you want to go, please stop at Katz's Delicatessen, since 1888 making legendary pastrami, corned beef and other Jewish deli classics. Other restaurant recommendations are Tavern on the Green, Il Mulino, La Grenouille, Nathan's Famous, Peter Luger, Sardi's, '21' Club, and Balthazar – best French onion soup I had in my entire life. I felt I was in Paris, I must admit. If you like onions, of course, you have to go there.

You probably know the tourist places that are a must-visit, like the Metropolitan Museum of Art, Empire State Building, Columbus Circle, World Trade Center, Central Park (yes, yes, yes), Guggenheim, MoMA, Time Square, Brooklyn Bridge, Grand Central Terminal, etc, etc. But there are sooooo many other cool things to do, like go to the High Line, one of my favorite places, and go to the Gallery Hopping in Chelsea, the Chelsea Market is wonderful, and visit the Smorgasburg on Kent Ave in Brooklyn. Every Saturday and Sunday from April through October, Smorgasburg showcases 100 local and regional food vendors. Best truffle fries in the world, I promise it's worth standing in line behind 100 people to try it. Seriously. And the ice-cream sandwich and the surf and turf burger.

Oh, just remembered something unforgettable, for me. And that might give you some courage to do something you want to do, even if the chances are tiny. My brother-in-law's sister lives two blocks away from Woody Allen's apartment, in Manhattan. So, one day, after leaving her house, and taking care of her kids, I took out of my backpack my resumé and headshots and sneaked into his building and just dropped them under his door. And ran away, like a scared cat. But then I stopped running and walked with a smile on my face. The chances were practically zero, but we never know if we never try, right? So, no, sorry, I can't say that he emailed me or gave me a call, or texted me, but I tried. Better than knowing where he lived and wanting to do it but never having the courage to do it, right?

One of my biggest flaws is too be too impulsive, which can be good if it's heading to focus, to work. But in life, in general, it isn't good. I got that from my mom and my dad, both very impulsive, but in different ways. My dad wants everything for yesterday, like there's no tomorrow. My mom is more impulsive in other things. So getting this from both of them, it was and it still is something I have to fight against and I talk to myself before taking action. Think before doing, not doing and then thinking. Courage is different. Courage is fighting against your fears and doing something that is good for you. Like I just told Woody's story. But impulsiveness isn't. I've still a lot to learn, but even at 26 years old and living four years abroad, I had to deal with my actions and the reactions it caused for me and other people. As long as we learn from our mistakes, recognize them, we are taking a step forward, and learning not to repeat them. That's what learn means, for me.

There's a balance in life that we need and are always in search to find. This balance lives within us. Outside and in other people isn't the place to look for it. It's here, inside our hearts and minds. The first step anyone must take is inward. The only person who can give you what you need and peace in your heart is your own true self, in the deep canyon of your soul. Find your value and worth, treat yourself well, respect what your heart, your body and soul are telling you, and don't let anyone, ever, put you down, when you know you did nothing wrong. But learn to apologize when you were wrong, when you created an unnecessary drama, or caused pain or said things impulsively that you regret. Don't let pride get in the way of being honest with yourself and your loved ones, because in the end, love is the answer. The love you carry in your chest, the love you give, the love you receive. Don't expect in return, don't create expectations, learn to have patience, little steps every day. Don't take steps bigger than you can, learn how to walk, then learn how to run to the things that make you happy.

I lived in Brooklyn for a couple of months on my second year in New York and I love it there. Williamsburg has so many cute and nice stores and bars, it's cozy and beautiful. Go and do non-tourist things too. Explore all you can, because NYC has so much to offer. I fell in love with the city, although it was a love/hate relationship. Sometimes I hated the cold, or sweating like a cow in the summer, and I hated having to walk with a thousand people around me, but I also loved it, the spring, the fall, going to bars with my friends, parks, and so on.

Two of the nicest people I met were Rose and Patti Ganguzza, two amazing producers. They welcomed me with love and every Sunday we used to go to Dim Sum Go Go in Chinatown and talk about movies, the industry, life in general. I also met Gabi Fleck, who used to work for Rose. She is Brazilian like me and a very smart, sweet girl who is also an actress. We became good friends.

Paloma Gabriel Cavalheiro, Gabi Fleck and Carolina Brandão are the three most determined young girls I've ever met. My childhood best friend, Laura Petracco, introduced me to Paloma after she moved to NYC. We shared some pretty good moments together, going to the movies and bars, and she was always straightforward with her advice for my love life. She compared me with Ted Mosby from *How I Met Your Mother* – if you have seen the show, you'll understand. Ted is an incurable romantic and dreamer. Carolina is the best producer I've known. She was starting her career in NYC but man, that girl had all it takes. She worked 12-14 hours a day and I admire her for giving so much to her career. Producing is for the tough and strong ones. Crazy hours, lots of paperwork, etc, etc. She is the type of friend who will be 100% honest and say when she doesn't agree with something you are doing, or you won't see for months because she's so busy, but when you really, really needed her, she was there. And Gabi is an incredible actress and singer. The three of them made my days in NYC much better and loving. And for that I will always be thankful.

I was lucky enough to meet one of my favorite

actresses, Cate Blanchett, after seeing her Broadway debut *The Present*. In my opinion, she's one of the best actresses in the world. But now I will have to list some of my other favorite actors. Top 50, this time: Meryl Streep (the queen), Cate Blanchett, Marion Cotillard, Melanie Laurent, Julianne Moore, Kristin Scott Thomas, Hilary Swank, Nicole Kidman, Jessica Chastain, Kate Winslet, Olivia Wilde, Emily Blunt, Michelle Williams, Carey Mulligan, Viola Davis, Uzo Aduba, Taylor Schilling, Emma Stone, Rachel McAdams, Angelina Jolie, Penélope Cruz, Natalie Portman, Reese Witherspoon, Amy Adams, Anne Hathaway, Julia Roberts, Sandra Bullock, Susan Sarandon, Helen Mirren, Judi Dench, Meg Ryan, Jennifer Aniston, Emma Thompson, Emma Watson, Angelina Jolie. Brazilian actors: Adriana Esteves, Marília Pêra, Fernanda Montenegro. And now the boys: Wagner Moura, Daniel Day-Lewis, Al Pacino, Robert De Niro, Kevin Spacey, Sean Penn, Tom Hanks, Denzel Washington, Morgan Freeman, Heath Ledger, Matthew McConaughey, Jake Gyllenhaal, Tom Hardy.

I could keep on going and name 100 amazing actors that inspired me, but I tried hard to keep to 50. I'd love to know what would be your list and why you love these actors. Yes, I am a very curious person. In Brazil there are many wonderful actors. Fernanda

Montenegro, who was once nominated for an Oscar, is our Brazilian actress queen. I have to admit that we do have soap operas in Brazil, and they are incredibly good. I wish the world could see a little bit of our work here. The quality of our work in soap operas is equivalent to American TV series. If only the world could see all the amazing things we have in our country.

Even though I don't feel at home in my own country, I know its value. I said before some things about Brazil but here it goes a bit more: We have the Amazon forest. We have one of the most beautiful islands in the world, Fernando de Noronha, the north of Brazil, the "Nordeste" with amazing beaches, Rio de Janeiro, "the wonderful city" as we call it, we have waterfalls, mountains, an immensity of natural beauty and the people. Brazilians can live with very little in the way of material wealth, but we will be friendly, we will laugh, we will reach out a helping hand to others who need us. Don't be afraid to come to Brazil. You need to be careful, as you might have to in so many other countries, but don't let that fear take away the opportunity to visit Brazil.

In 2015, during one of my visits to Brazil, my sister was sitting on the couch at my mom's home and she said: "Laura, I have something to tell you." I sat next to her. She looked serious, and I was afraid she was going to be angry at me for something I didn't even know I did, but she said: "You are going to be an auntie again".

"What? Really? Oh my god, that's amazing news!" I said. She interrupted me and said: "But you're gonna have two nephews. I'm pregnant with twins."

TWINS! Unbelievable. That tiny body of hers was carrying my two nephews. I can't even explain what my face must have looked like, but my eyes must have been the same size as Scrat's from the Ice Age films, that acorn-crazy saber-toothed squirrel. I was jumping around in such a state of happiness and bliss. My sister wanted to have another baby so much. She had lost one before having Mari and another one after her, so, let me tell you, I really do believe that there's a reason for things, and those two babies that weren't born were now coming. She was already in her 13th week of pregnancy, so things were going well, she just needed to rest a lot and not move too much during the whole pregnancy. It wasn't easy. She couldn't give full attention to Mari, but Renato, my brother-in-law, was always loving and present and Mari understood and was happy to know she was going to have two little brothers.

After staying a month back in Brazil with them and enjoying that beautiful news, helping my sister out and with my niece and mom and friends, I went back to NYC. Back to classes. November 3rd, 2015, I received a call in the middle of the class from my mom. She usually texted me, so I knew it was something important. I asked my teacher's permission to leave and answered the phone. There was a lot of noise around in the building so I went outside, in the cold, and my mom said: "Laura, your sister is on her way to the hospital, the boys are going to be born now."

She was only seven and a half months pregnant, so it was risky, it was scary. My friend Bruna Burmeister was there at the time, so I called her and she ran to find me and hug me, and be my shoulder to cry on. We prayed together. All that day I spent praying for the boys to be OK, to be healthy.

They were born at a weight of three pounds (1.3kg), so tiny. They went straight to the Intensive Care Unit (ICU) and spend 50 days there, attached to machines.

My sister would go every single day to take care of her new little boys, to sing songs for them, to pray for them, to feed them. My sister is my hero. And after those 50 days, she went to the hospital with my brother-in-law and my niece to bring them home. They brought more love, more joy, more happiness to our entire family. They went through really difficult times, but both of them were soon getting plump and smiling and playing. They have had all the love in this world from my sister, my brother-in-law, my niece, and us.

My mom and me. The whole family. Two little Scorpios – yep, since they were born earlier than they should have, they got the tough sign, Scorpio, same as my sister. They were supposed to be Sagittarius like their auntie, but it is what it is. They are and will always be the best gift life gave me, and my niece, Mariana.

Jo was like a mom to me when I was born, at 16 years old. I might not remember all the nights she put me to sleep, read stories for me, but I cannot be thankful enough for all the love she gave to me, more than a sister – she was a second mom to me. And she taught me so much about life, about what really matters, about respect - about trust, about honesty, about honor, and unconditional love.

Chapter 10

Auditions and Expeditions

Now I had my degree in acting. After getting my degree in film-making in my city in Brazil, I now had a degree in acting in New York City. But I had no job and one year to "make it", to find a sponsor for another type of visa to be able to stay longer, to audition 20 times a day, to spend nights awake on backstage.com, castingnetworks.com and countless other websites to find auditions for short movies, commercials, student films, plays or anything to add in the resume and keep working. It's hard to be a foreigner. If it's already hard to make it as an actor when you are American, imagine being NOT from America. Twice as hard. Not complaining, just sharing.

I came back from Brazil and went straight to LA. Something inside me was saying that I should try it out back in LA, since now I had the Working Visa – why not go back to where everything started and start auditioning there? Also, I could be close to Cintia and Lana, my two angels. Cintia was the one that took care of me when I had the appendicitis, and she is my soul sister. I never knew such a big heart as hers, a person who is always wanting to help others. And Lana is a little copy of her, the sweetest, the most joyful little angel I've met. I was so happy to have them around.

Plus, two of my best friends were also in LA, Rafael Stiborski and Dani Heindrich. They both flew from other cities to be with me during my graduation ceremony. I don't know what my life would have been without those two and Cintia.

They stood by my side even when I got all dramatic and sad or did things I shouldn't do. It didn't matter where I was, I could always call, share my struggles with them. We lived crazy, happy moments together, and also difficult ones. We shared stories, sorrows, as we all have a big thing in common: We are crazy lovers about life and traveling. Friends like these I want to keep for the rest of my life, until we are old ladies (or old gentlemen).

I was happy and excited to be back in LA and seeing my old friends. I knew it was going to be tough, since I would have to spend more money and buy a car, something I wouldn't have to do in NYC. But there was I, buying on Craigslist the second version of my Johnny Bravo – yes, my car had a name – a 2002 Mitsubishi Pajero/Montero. When I was living in LA in 2013, I had my first Johnny, a 1997 version. He lasted well, though, some issues here and there but he was a champ. He survived eight trips – LA to San Francisco, back and forth – in a year. That's something to be proud of. I did those trips back in 2013, when my mom came to visit me, my sister, brother-in-law and niece, and another four or five trips with friends from LA and others that came from Brazil to visit. This is one of the reasons I love California so much, the Big Sur: Highway 1.

"We've been on the run, driving in the sun
looking out for number one
California here we come
right back where we started from,
Californiaaaaaaaaa, here we come"
- *Composed by the band Phantom Planet.*

That's a song by Phantom Planet. I loved that show when I was a teenager, it was the intro to *The OC*. And it was part of my life's soundtrack living in California.

I stayed in LA from June until December with my new Johnny, driving around, working my ass off to help pay the bills, going to auditions and more auditions, trying to write some scenes and do it with some actor's friends.

I did talk about OPT, how difficult it is to be a foreigner in American, or a foreigner in any country. But if you are going to follow this career as actor, you will have to learn to fall, and get back on your knees every day. Keep practicing, keep going to classes, improv, scene study, workshops, but don't stop. Connections in this industry is so important, you might meet your agent, producer for your next project in a class, or even at a bar, or in one of the workshops you did, without expecting that to happen. In LA and NYC I sometimes had four auditions a day, or some days no auditions, just preparing myself for them. It's one profession where you will hear 'no' a lot of times, but you cannot give up if it's what you really want. These no's will only make you stronger and the best way to learn as an actor is to practice, practice and practice more and more. So many people give up just because they get tired of receiving so many no's. Sometimes they don't even get to finish the audition, they just cut you out and call 'next'. It happened to me 100 times or more, literally. Does that mean you are a bad actor? No! My teachers kept repeating to me: "You are gonna go out there, and you are going to cry, take the elevator down after the audition and say, "Damn, why I didn't do it this way or that way? Why I didn't wear a pink shirt instead of blue? And 20 more questions buzzing in your mind. And you will feel shitty, and the next day shittier, but then some days you'll get out of the audition and say to yourself: "Good job, dude". Because you felt good. You didn't worry so much about what others would think. You didn't let your anxiety speak louder, you just said "fuck it, let's do this" and did it. Maybe your hair wasn't how they wanted, maybe you were too short for that role, and you got a "no" again, but if you did a good job, they WILL remember you, maybe not for this role, but for another one. Your work will start to appear in casting meetings, every audition, every role you do will introduce you to more people. And during an audition you might or might not get the call back, if you do get it, it's a good sign even if you don't end up getting that role, or you might get it. BOOM! All those things can happen. But that day when you hear, 'You got the part! You got the role!' That day will come. Cheers to the good, the bad and the should have. You fail, and you will rise again, my friend.

So failing is part of our craft. And there were successes, some nice, surprising roles I got that I never expected. One day I auditioned for a spec commercial in LA. First of all, there were four buildings, and I got there an hour before my audition time, and waited, and waited, and only 15 minutes before the audition I asked the receptionist: Is this the place for the commercial test? Answer: "No. It's in building number 2, you are in number 4." I thought, "Fuck! Now I am almost late" and ran to the other building, and no, it wasn't number 2, it was number 3. So, I got there, finally, in the right building, all sweaty and thankfully, the casting directors still waited for me. Which I was really thankful for, but the dudes didn't even let me finish my three lines. They stopped me on my first and said: "Thank you. We will contact you if we think you are a good fit."

Well, great. Thanks, I thought as I left. It's OK, I was out of breath, exhausted, and sad, because they didn't even let me finish my three-line audition. Was I that bad? Or they were punishing me for being late? I don't know. I will never know. So, what I am trying to say here is that you will go through this (maybe not exactly this, hopefully not, I do not wish that for you), but those things can happen and you have to get used to it. Rejection, being rejected, is part of our lives as actors.

There are so many examples of actors that took a

long time to succeed. I don't know if you like Mark Ruffalo, I do. But he is a great example. Mark was rejected from 600 auditions before his career took off when in the film *You Can Count on Me* he finally played the troubled brother of Laura Linney (yes, I just need an 'e' and a 'y' at the end, but I am just Laura Linn, not famous, yet, just a big dreamer and passionate about my craft). Ruffalo said, "All these casting directors were like, 'Where did you come from?' and I'm like, 'What are you talking about? I've been under your noses for the past 10 years! Where have *you* been?'" He went on: 'It's been mythologized now but it started with about 600 auditions without success. Most smart people would have quit when it takes that long." Just don't quit! Easy to say that, difficult to not do it, because we all need to survive. But if you have a side job and acting is your real deal and dream, keep trying. Your day will come. "The only failure is not to try" – George Clooney.

Another experience to share was a super good moment and at the same time awful. Why? I will explain. I did one of those programs where you meet tons of casting directors, producers, agents, it was a great way to put yourself into the movie industry there. Making connections – something you have to do as an actor. Always communicating, changing ideas, contacts, you need to get your butt out of bed and go do things. I also made new friends there, some of whom I still talk too. We created a nice group of people, and we were able to present monologues and scenes for casting directors and agents. For some film/TV series agents in NYC, I had to do a sci-fi monologue which they gave to me based on my short hair, my looks and what my "type" could be. I wasn't passionate about the monologue at first sight, but that's what they gave me and they probably knew much better than I did what my scene should be to present to them, to maybe, maybe, one day get a call, or sign a contract... who knows?

I was number 16 on the list to go to the audition room with those five big agents. Legs shaking, the actors running from one side to other, working on their lines, focusing, praying, breathing, doing yoga, all that. I went to the hall to practice and went to the bathroom to breathe and say to myself in the mirror: "Just do it. Believe you can do it. It's only gonna be five minutes of your life, or more or less, and that's it. You can't control what they will think, or if they will like it, you worked on this scene, so just go and do it".

I left the bathroom and I guess they were already on number 13 or 14, so almost my time to go, and one of the actors left crying and so, so sad and I said, "Wow, are you OK?" I gave her a hug and she was super upset because they weren't nice to her or simply didn't like her and gave her their critiques and notes. I was the next or almost the next, so I told her we would talk later. Seeing her crying like that just made me more scared and desperate, but I said again to myself: *No, no, no, Laura. Focus. It's your turn. Don't let your anxiety take over you again, like most of the times it did.* And I literally said "Fuck it." Three times. Not loudly, but whispering. "Fuck it, fuck it, fuck it. I am going to enter that room and just do what I know and feel and that's fucking it." Lots of cursing I know, but sometimes it's a good way. At least for me.

Well, I did it. And then I was there, sitting quietly and they were making notes and then looking at me. Each of them had a paper to make notes about headshots, resume, overall comments, presentation & appearance, etc. I was quite happy with the notes, even though some of them mentioned some things I should change in my resume, or do new headshots. One of the agents said to me: "Laura, you were the first one, since we sat in this room to see your performances, that really woke me up. That really made me interested. And I couldn't take my eyes off you". Those were the words, because that was like the biggest compliment I ever got. "This type of monologue and character really fits for you," he said.

Then he asked: "You are American, right?"

I said, "No, I am from Brazil". And he and the other

four were surprised to hear that because one of the others said, "Well, good job, because I didn't hear any accent, and that's a big step for someone who's not from here". Then the guy said: "Well, I would like to get in contact with you, but do you have the O-1 Visa?"

Boom! I said: "No, I don't". Fuck, I thought to myself. And they said: "Thank you, Laura. It was really nice meeting you, great job, keep on going and try to get that O-1, girl".

I am not saying I would have got a contract with one of them, but that's why I said it was an amazing experience, but also bad. Because finally, after some showcases and acting programs I did to meet casting directors and agents, I had someone that wanted to maybe be my agent, and that is wonderful, BUT – I didn't have the O-1. And I didn't have enough material to apply for one yet. I only had six more months of my OPT visa and it was simply not happening at that time. So, bad and good, right?

I had my bad days, the days I wanted to just give up or think, *why am I still doing this? Why do I want to be an actor?* And I was far away from my family, my niece and nephew and friends. I was freaking out because my visa would expire and I wouldn't be able to work legally and I would never, ever, want to stay in a country illegally. I spent days thinking about all those things, but I didn't let that put me down or give up.

I knew why I wanted to be an actor. Because it makes me feel alive, it's like I am falling in love every single time I do a scene, a monologue, I feel those butterflies, the same we feel when we go on a first promising date. You know? I was one of millions of actors pursuing it and trying it. But it was worth it, and still is. If my future was going to be in the USA, Brazil, China or Australia, that didn't matter, as long as I was working with what I loved.

Some advice I can give you: watch movies, watch documentaries, read plays, read books, travel, take every experience in, as many as you can. Rehearse scenes, even if you aren't able to do classes at the moment where you are now, do a monologue to someone, a friend or a member of your family, make your reel with the work you've done so far, or grab your friends, write a script and make videos, ask questions about your character, do your research, keep practicing, and remember that it is not about you, it's about the other person, it's about the story being told. Don't get caught in your thoughts, or how you plan the scene, moves, etc, because when you enter the audition room, you have to leave your problems at the door. Do your work and don't overthink, you need to be present. Be fully committed. Roll with it. Listen! Listen! What you expect, trained before entering the room can change completely once you enter there. Learn to take directions from what has been asking of you, be adaptable, and own your space, be professional. Focus. Don't ever judge the character you are playing, try to understand him, otherwise you won't be able to connect truthfully. Allow yourself to be open. Great things will come out of it if you simply do your work before and right then, in the audition room.

"Giving voice to characters that have no other voice – that's the great worth of what we do." – Meryl Streep

Chapter 11

Breakthrough

There's this Brazilian song in my mind all day long that says: "Live and don't be ashamed to be happy, sing and sing and sing the beauty of being an eternal learner". In Portuguese it would be: *Viver e não ter a vergonha de ser feliz, cantar e cantar e cantar a beleza de ser um eterno aprendiz.* It goes on, "We are on this earth to grow, to love and to enjoy the beauty of being a learner, always. Never take for granted what you have today, and the people in your life. Go, be happy, happiness is moments, memories, simple little things, not an eternal state."

I came back to Brazil for Christmas 2016, and we

spent New Year in my sister's house at the beach in Florianópolis. And then at the beginning of January I went back to NYC. I wanted to try the last six months of my OPT there. I had tried in LA, now I was going to try in NYC. But something amazing happened – an opportunity I wasn't expecting. In July 2016, a guy called Andre Frauenstein added me on Facebook. OK, we had one friend in common, Reine Swart, who had also studied at NYFA back in 2010. She is South African and such a talented actress. Andre send me a message through my acting page on Facebook saying:

Hi Laura, I am the producer of Siembamba, in which Reine plays the lead. My company is www.phoenixfilms.co.za for easy reference, would like to make contact for future collaborations, if possible? Regards, Andre.

We kept in touch, talking from time to time, and once he said: "Laura, I have this feeling that I need to work with you, that you should be in one of our feature films and future projects, I don't know why, I just know." That's why I say that things happen for a reason and there are two magic ingredients in life: luck and fate. We kept talking and he knew I'd never done a feature movie before but I told him he would have the best of me if he chose me to be in one of his productions.

He talked about a script they were writing, the story of a runner in the desert. He asked me to film myself running (I was in Florianópolis, not in my best shape, but my brother-in-law helped me and we filmed at the beach, so I was running in the sand). I sent the video to him and didn't hear from Andre for a few days. When I was already back in New York, he messaged me that he and his crew liked the video and saw potential. He sent me the script when I was in NYC, and we talked on Skype. "I might be talking to the future Tatiana Magalhães" he said. They had created this character, a Brazilian runner, who would be a supporting role in the movie.

As soon as he sent me the script, I started reading it. I spent seven hours lying on the couch reading it and recording notes – he asked me to do that. But he also asked me to read not only as Tatiana, but as the lead character of the movie. So I did. And I fell in love with that script. My heart was beating fast and I was crying, because I was so, so moved by the story. Somehow, for a moment, all my insecurities were gone, because during my recording audios and notes, I said: "Andre, I am happy if you give me the character of Tatiana, but I was born to do this woman, Mary Harris".

I recorded some of the dialogues in the audio notes and sent them to him. Three days later he asked me on Facebook Messenger: "Laura, do you have five minutes to talk on Skype?" I was running late for an audition, but I said "of course". We talked and the first thing he said was: "We all listened to the audio that you sent and the notes, and we feel you are the one, so welcome aboard, Laura, you are now the lead character of our movie".

I burst into tears of joy. I couldn't believe my dream was coming true. All those years studying, all the auditions, all the bad and good days, it was all worth it. I had known that one day I would have a chance to show my talent and my effort, that someday a person would see something unique in me, as every one of us has. Andre saw that in me.

He said, "You will need to work hard, you are going to interpret a runner, so you need to start right away, training, getting ready".

"Yes, sir." I was ready to start my preparation.

I talked to my parents about the movie and they were so happy for me. I knew it wasn't going to be easy, I would have to lose a lot of weight, train every day, get my psyche ready, get a six-pack. So I made the decision to go back to Brazil earlier. I wanted to be close to my family and friends to have their support, because it was going to be tough, so on March 2nd I flew back to Porto Alegre. Home sweet home.

Then I started my biggest challenge in life so far,

physically and emotionally. I was pushing myself every day, in a battle with my deepest thoughts and feelings. Changes. My life turned upside down, in a good way. March 8th 2017 was the day I started training and prepping for my first feature movie as an actor. The script went through a lot of changes, and my character at that time was named Mary Harris. It was produced by Phoenix Films, a production company from South Africa, and directed by Darrell Roodt, Oscar nominee for the movie *Yesterday* in 2005 and the director of *Sarafina* with Whoopi Goldberg, among many other movies. I was beyond happy to work with a director like him. Just the title of the movie gives me goosebumps: *The Furnace*. Our movie. It's really a dream come true.

For all these years I had been studying hard, living abroad, working early every day, sleeping late, dreaming with my characters, the plays I was doing, moment to moment, character to character. I had been living day by day, knowing each one of them, learning their story, connecting to their feelings, their lives, their fears and goals, going to class, being taught by the best teachers and mentors, some of whom pushed me further than I could ever have imagined I could go. But I did. Moments of weakness, of tears, of fear of the unknown. Moments where something hidden inside of me suddenly awakened, rose and shone, arose from the darkness to light my inner self. Acting – what is it? What is it that drives us to be actors? It's not acting. It's telling the truth. It's diving into the immense complexity of our inner selves, it's the excitement of making that story, that person, part of us. And then sharing it with the world.

Every single character becomes part of us. After a while, we have to let them all go, somehow; because, at the end of the day, we still are one, a person with their own life, desires, thoughts, dreams, but those stories, those people, we gave them life. We took them from a play, a script, a story, and put them into action. Do all your research, read, see, imagine all that the character went through, the people he/she loved, what makes them want to keep living, their issues, their loved ones, the background. Create their past; what's his favorite color? What does his house look like? How was her childhood, relationship with friends and family, first love? Even if it's not written in the script, you have to know them, to *be* them, represent them truthfully. Memorize the lines, but that's less than one per cent of the job; our job as actors starts *after* knowing the lines as our own, knowing them without even thinking about them. That's where our journey begins, after going into their deepest selves.

And then, you forget about it. All of it. That way you will be able to be present in that moment, in that scene. In that second. And know that acting isn't about you, it's about the other person, the one you are talking to at that specific moment. It's about that silent, non-speaking, voiceless instant that tells more than words. The look in your eyes. The breath, the emotion present in that split of a second. Don't try to act, perform; don't worry about being big, whether it's on a stage or on a screen. Be truthful, real and honest and the rest will come. The rest will take care of itself, if you live it fully.

How lucky I am to be me and at the same time all those people who are somewhere inside me. Those people and stories that made me grow, that taught me so much about life, feelings, suffering, pain, love, happiness.

After all these adventures, discoveries, classes, lessons, I was now heading to the biggest one so far. I was blessed to have this opportunity. All professions must be respected. All of them take hard work, but in acting, not only do you need to be determined and never give up, even after a year or two without work – so many actor friends that I know are doing side jobs because acting doesn't pay the bills – or receiving "no's" and more "no's" from casting directors, auditions, etc, but you also need talent *and* luck – yes, luck is important, besides all the determination and effort. And luck is something you can't really control. Most things in life we cannot control.

But when a big opportunity knocks on your door, go see what it is, take the risk, if your heart tells you it's the right thing to do. This I want to say: always follow your instincts. I know how lucky I am to have the chance to do my first feature movie. I lie down in bed every day and say "thank you" to the universe for giving me this opportunity because there are so, so, so many talented people in this world, and sometimes they do not have a chance, to find someone that truly *sees* them and wants to give them a real opportunity.

So I headed into this journey, preparing myself with all my heart. It is the journey of a woman who loses her loved ones, her strength to run, who has respiratory failure after a huge accident, and finds her path to make this huge breakthrough. Her love for running is still there, and that gives her the strength to keep on trying, but she has to go through a huge healing process internally and externally to be at peace with herself. From one day having all you love, even with the obstacles and pain situations every human being has, to another day where suddenly everything falls apart. Where hope is lost. Where the dream seems now so far out of reach. Where your loved one are gone and there's no way back.

I fell in love with this woman, with this character, with her story, every day a bit more. Every day she became closer to me, part of me. I was diving into this big unknown, undiscovered foreign land and reality. A runner, a seeker, not only as a professional runner, but running against all odds, running towards her truth and leaving behind the guilt that she carries in her shoulders and in her heart, like a thousand rocks. I saw Mary Harris, I felt her. I understood her. When you don't have strength anymore to run, you have to find that strength in your heart, because that's where passion lives.

Let's talk about the physical preparation. I had to physically change from eight to 80 in those few months, embody her lifestyle. And this transformation is not only physical but mental, as well. You need to change the way you think, you have to believe that you can do it. Not only try, but actually do it. Don't try to eat healthier – *be* healthier. Don't try to go to the gym thinking it's a difficult thing, go and do your best. Whatever your goal is, stick to it, commit to it, give 100% of you. Once you are committed to something, whatever that is, don't give up on yourself and your beliefs. Believe in yourself. Believe in your power of change. Believe in your power of growth. We all have self-doubt, we all have insecurities, fears, but don't let that stop you from going further. The best internal dialogue you can have is with your heart, when your mind starts doubting. Because it's in your heart that your dreams, passions and desires live. And there's no doubt inside your heart if you truly listen to it.

Feeling good about yourself is such an important thing and it's so easy to get lost, to go to extremes, but I learned to put my health on first, before anything else, mentally and physically.

Slowly, I found my self-love, my self-esteem. So when this movie came, I knew it was going to be harsh. I'd have to lose all that weight to portrait a runner in the desert, but I was determined and ready for it. I lost 16kg in total, but in a healthy way and with the support of professionals, my amazing nutritionist Roberta Sant'Anna Volkart and my personal trainer, Marcia Ghignatti. I had to face my own fears and insecurities as Laura, and let my character in, with her own fears, pain, love and desires.

We have the willpower to get away from things that aren't good for us. Addictions: alcohol, smoking, other drugs, as well as people, toxic people, relationships. We all have that willpower hidden somewhere, we just need to find it inside us, and be persistent with ourselves.

It's hard to get away from something that is already a habit for us – a specific person, job, addictions in general. We get used to having that someone or something in our daily lives, even if we are conscious how bad it is for us. So it all comes down to how much you really want something. How much are you willing to fight, suffer if needed to get through that? To live a better life?

After three months of daily exercises, gym, eating healthy, I finally achieved this huge goal for me, to lose so much weight, to follow what I was asked to follow to do my character, even if now everything had changed. And that can happen in a movie. On July 19th 2017, two months before I was going to South Africa to shoot the movie I'd been preparing for over the past months, I open my email, as I do every day, and there was one from my producer. The title of the email: *The Furnace* (the name for the movie, the suggestion the distributors gave). I opened the email, hoping for good news. They were having some financial issues and that was the reason the movie had been postponed

I started reading the first words:

"Dear Laura, it is with the utmost regret that we have to inform you that we have to cancel the movie in its existing form."

I stopped it there. I couldn't breathe and I literally couldn't keep reading the email, because the shock was so big that I felt completely overwhelmed and paralyzed. I closed my eyes and breathed deeply, saying to myself: "It's OK, Laura". I kept on reading. It explained why they needed to cancel – the investors weren't interested in the story as it was written, they wanted changes.

Number three of the four things they wanted to change was that they wanted an American actress to portray the lead character.

I burst into tears. I closed the email and went to my mom's room. I literally fell on the floor and couldn't stop crying and couldn't breathe properly. Exaggerating? I wouldn't say so, it was my heart and my reaction to it, after all those months of training, all those months of dedication, focus, commitment to my character and how to embody her, a complete surrender, emotionally and physically. I repeat 'physically' here because it was a real drastic change to embody this character, as I have written. I had delivered everything they asked for. I had been losing weight since the first month, but slowly, because my body was readapting to a total different life style. They asked me to lose 6kg, and I did. Then, a month or two before we were to start shooting (the date based on the contract was May 28th to start shooting) they said: "You need to lose 10 more kilos based on your pictures." And I did it.

I went for it. I didn't just get close but just as they asked me: "make the impossible possible". I made it happen. I felt exhausted, tired, weak, but I lost the 10kg. Total 16kg in less than three months. And for the last one I maintained and kept exercising to tone my body, my muscles.

In the movie industry a lot can change, dates, etc, but I wasn't expecting this. This subject was never on the table. I talked to my producer almost every week for updates and how the process of getting the investors was going. Now the reality was that I had two options. One was for them to pay a settlement fee and the other would be to give me a supporting role in the movie still. One of the two.

I spent the entire day thinking. I wasn't the only one in shock. My friends and family were also devastated and didn't understand why and how this had happened. I had studied film-making, so I have an idea that it's not in their hands sometimes; as a production company they need investors to make a movie, financial support, and they need to show results in order to have the investment.

So having a Brazilian actress portraying an American lead in a South African movie wasn't the best choice, and I had to breathe and use my rational side. Even with the frustration and sadness, it was not in my hands. And it wasn't their fault at all.

I had a friend who worked months to do a leading role in a soap opera and a few days before shooting they changed her role. And the turnout at the end was actually amazing. She said everything happens for a reason, and I am 100% with her on that. As I have said many times, I am not a known actress, I am not an

Oscar nominee, but I am so grateful for the chance to do my work with such an amazing director that I deeply admire, Darrell, and work with such talented actors as Luthuli Dlamini, Thandi Puren, Armand Aucamp and Jamie Bernadette, the lead actress who will portray Mary Harris in The Furnace. She has worked in many feature movies and was most recently seen on NCIS: New Orleans. I've spoken to her a few times through message. She is a sweet and humble person and I am more than honored and looking forward to working with such a talented actress as her. I'll be doing my character with love and grace. We need to learn from frustrations and what is given to us. Dealing with changes and how we react to them is challenging, but very important, in fact essential.

The biggest frustration and disappointment was the way I received this news and how much I gave to this journey. I left NYC, by choice, to come to Brazil to be around family and friends, to have more emotional support, and I knew that being back home also I would have a better training, I would feel more comfortable to be uncomfortable, if that makes sense. I do not regret it at all. Because I did my work, for four months and 11 days since day one when I moved to Brazil, and got the script, I worked hard every single day to get where they wanted me to be for this character, emotionally and physically. I did my research, I found a coach to work with, I found a training gym, personal trainers, nutritionist, doctors to come along with me in this journey and find and give the best results I could. And I trained two hours a day, almost every day at the gym, I started running again after such a long period without running, not only to help lose weight but to feel it. I participated in two known runs in my city, to feel the energy, to know what it feels like to be in a running competition, the environment, the feeling of running with other people but still being by yourself. Because running is you against yourself, it's not about others, it's your focus, your energy and your performance. I studied running, I talked to ultra-marathon runners to know what it's like to run in the desert or such a long-distance marathon as 280km, something similar to what my character would go through. And that's my job. It's my job as an actor to fully understand what my character is going through and will go through. To feel in my skin the suffering, the power, the losses and achievements, the fears and dreams. However, it's not my job to control anything, so I had my first big chance to do this lead character that I really worked my ass off and then, it faded away.

But I do believe that "with every disappointment comes an opportunity." So I held on tight to my belief. I fell, I cried, but I got up even fiercer, stronger and with even more faith.

I replied to them saying that I would gladly accept the supporting role, not only because it was a great thing just to be part of the movie, work with a director that I really admired, knowing how much I would learn from it. Every experience counts, in front of the camera and behind the camera. The backstage as I would call it is our lives as actors, all that we go through, the preparation when we do get a role, the internal growth and acceptance when we do not, the endless lesson to keep on going, to accept all the "no's" and work and improve as actors. As people.

But I also said in an honest way, with my heart, how much I had dedicated to this movie, to this character. How I had spent almost five months immersed in her world, to get to know her. I did lose opportunities, invitations to do other acting jobs, and I refused them because my priority was the movie.

So my breakthrough wasn't as planned, but maybe it was supposed to happen in a different way, so all I could do was find peace and serenity, deal with the circumstances as they were. They could have just taken me out of the movie entirely and paid me a fee, but that's not how they are. Since day one when I started to talk with Andre, I knew and felt a connection, honesty, people with good hearts and from good faith. When we talked on Skype, July 21st, he wanted to know how I was doing and how I was dealing with this big change. I could sense that his words came from the heart when he said they wanted me in the movie, but they needed the investors in order to make it happen. He knew all the effort I had put in during those months.

So they decided to rewrite the script for me to have scenes of impact and a character that would help me start my career and show what I had to offer as an actor. As the quote says, "When a door closes, another one opens". I do believe in that. So no, my breakthrough is not as the lead of the movie, but as a supporting role. That changes things? No. I will still do my job, give 100% and accept that the universe wanted it this way, that this is the way I will start my career internationally. That's why I say that some doors close in order for others to open and everything happens in the right time.

During the transition, I got invited to shoot a teaser for a TV show called *3 Seconds Before Dying*, directed by Paulo Nascimento. The show had a teaser already, all in Portuguese, but it was refused. They tried and showed the script/idea of the project to the USA and other countries and they were super interested. So, the idea was to shoot another teaser, but this time in English. However, the actors who did the first teaser in Portuguese did not speak English very well, or without the Brazilian accent, so, my agent in Brazil passed my information, website, reel (in English) and resumé to one of the casting directors in São Paulo.

They really liked it, they saw that I didn't have a strong Brazilian accent, so they instantly put me in the project.

We had our rehearsal on August 4th and 5th and we shot the entire teaser in an abandoned house in Novo Hamburgo, a city close to Porto Alegre, where I live, in Brazil. So a door opened for me. If the movie in South Africa had happened in May-June as was the plan at the beginning, I wouldn't have had the chance to be part of this other project. I met such incredible and talented people. Paulo Nascimento is one of our best directors in Brazil and I've always admired his work. Will the project will be approved and shoot all next year? We still don't know. All I know is that I could do my job, make contacts, show my work and effort, and that is already a beginning. So, everything happens at the right time, that's one more proof of that for me.

The TV show is kind of supernatural. It's about the emissaries of death that follow people who are about to die, and we, the three emissaries, talk to the person who's about to die and all that happens in those three seconds before dying, the choices that people can make, and each episode is focused on a different story and person. I have my fingers crossed for the project to be successful and approved.

We try to control things, but so little is in our hands

to control. If you took your focus, if you gave your best and know that, and are always searching for enhancement, refining your skills, you can be sure that those doors will open for you. As they are slowly opening for me.

The actor's work does not start on the day we start filming. It starts on the first read of the script, the first connections and emotions. It starts when you allow yourself to risk, to believe in yourself and your power, your talent and do your best. That's what I've been doing every single day, since I first read the script and fell in love so deeply with the story, with the dialogue, with other characters and my own.

Our job is not something we do alone. As actors we also depend, thankfully, on an amazing group of talented people: the scriptwriter, the director, the producers, the other actors, every single person from the crew that also makes this journey. And that is how we make a movie. Together. Doing our job, with all we got. How thankful I am to have this door open, an opportunity, a sign that someone saw in me, believed in my capability and now we are making it happen.

So hopefully, soon, you'll know more about this movie, this journey of a Brazilian actress who is having the chance to make her first feature movie internationally. South Africa, wild animals, big production – my biggest dream coming true.

The year 2017 brought so many changes to my life, and such growth. In 2017 I moved back to Brazil, after four years living abroad and just coming to Brazil to visit my family and my friends. I physically changed so much, losing weight, gaining muscles, changing my eating habits and diet. I quit smoking. I fell in love again with the same person I fell in love with years before and it was worth it. I wrote this, my first book. I composed my first song. And I am about to do my first feature movie as an actress.

It's incredible how things happen exactly how they should, and that is just the truth. I do believe we have paths in life and we can make our own choices, but some things we just can't control, they are bigger than us and when they happen, after a while, you realize that it makes perfect sense. Even if at the time, it didn't make any sense and you felt completely lost.

The Furnace is one of the biggest examples of things that unfold in the right way. When I first described the journey and how I got the leading role, I said that at first, I was supposed to do the supporting role, a Brazilian runner. And after all this training, all the changes, here I am, in a new supporting role for the same movie. It was truly a roller coaster, with a lot of ups and downs and feeling the butterfly in my stomach. But in the end, this is exactly how it was meant to be. This is the best solution for the movie, for everyone involved, including me. I felt my heart breaking into pieces when I got the email saying I wasn't the lead anymore, but this wasn't the producer's fault, or anyone's fault. They wanted a true American actress for the role and someone who already had a name, and I am not that girl yet. Maybe someday. But as Andre said: "I think this is going to be a very challenging role for you and the best way of breaking onto the big screen circuit". He is right. The main thing is to do my job, to dive into the character and the story, fall in love with her, do what I have to do, and the rest will take care of itself. Doesn't matter if I am the lead, supporting role or just a grain of sand in the middle of the desert. Doesn't matter the size of the role, what matters is to do your job with everything you've got. Give your heart, mind and soul to what has been giving it to you. We are all unique in our own way and our star will shine in the right time, in the right way, we can't rush things.

When I first read the new script, which I finally got by August 2017, I was so thankful and touched by it. Darrell Roodt, the director of the movie, could have created a supporting role that didn't have much impact in the story, but no, he thought and wrote the new script carefully, adding an important element to the plot: faith. And with faith, my character was created.

How lucky am I to do this. To immerse myself in a role that overflows with love. When I was reading the script, I could see Rafaela in front of me, I could already see the scenes, somehow, and even knowing how challenging it would be for me, I knew it was "destiny" in my life, as Laura, to do Rafaela. And when you accept things how they are, an internal peace takes over you. That doesn't mean you are not fighting for what you really want, because you are, but you are not swimming upstream. Every opportunity is worth it. It's not about how big a role is, but what you make out of it.

October 2nd 2017 I took my flight to South Africa. Our movie was postponed to March 2018, but my friend who was going with me for the shooting had already bought her flight ticket. No refund, so I decided that it would be a great idea actually to go early, to meet Andre Frauenstein, my producer, his dear wife, Elbie, and Samuel, their son and producer at Phoenix Films. Plus, I had the opportunity to meet Darrell Roodt, my director. I spoke with Andre on Skype and he thought it was a great idea. Instead of just jumping out of the plane straight to the set in March, going now, even not shooting the film, I would be able to get a better feeling about the people I would work with, and get to know South Africa, the history about the country, culture, politics, etc.

It's hard to put into words what this trip was to me, and to my friend, Rovena. I was nervous, butterflies in my stomach, but in a good way. It was going to be the first time I would meet them in person since the start of the pre-production and our talks were only through Facebook, Messenger, What's App, emails, skype, etc.

Rovena actually arrived two days before and was working hard on her English, but it was a big challenge for her. She was afraid she wouldn't be able to communicate that well. Which was completely normal, specially with strangers. But as soon as she got to the airport, Elbie and Andre were there waiting for her with open arms and open hearts. Then, two days after, the three of them picked me up at the airport. The first hug I gave to them, my heart was filled with love already and a sensation that I was coming home, as well. If I had good thoughts and expectations about them, I can say, I left South Africa with ten times more love, more belief, more certainty that this was the right path we were heading to and that not only I was making my first feature movie with them, but I was meeting people I want to keep for the rest of my life and as we all said, we became family.

Andre and Elbie welcomed us to their house, in Gauteng, close to Johannesburg. When I got there, we actually went straight to Kruger Park, a four-hour drive. A quick nap in the car was necessary but then, with the best songs and soundtracks that Andre played all trip, it was hard to not stay awake and enjoy the view, the music and their company.

I've never met such gentle kind people. I felt safe and with my heart warm, protected. Andre is a big fan of jokes and loves to make fun of me. He said: "You are so easy to fool, Laura". In a good way. So, we "hit the road, Jack". Writing this, every single thing, I remember those exact moments and wish I could go back.

We got to Kruger Park on October 3rd, evening. One of the biggest surprises was they booked us an incredible place, a tent to sleep in. And, of course, a big fireplace outside for "braai", their famous barbecue in South Africa. They had friends staying in another tent nearby, so, we went there. We ate so much food, and so many wonderful drinks. Rovena said the best phrase of the night: "Where is God? Because I think I am in paradise." Couldn't have said it any better. We sat around the fire, eating and listening to music and looking at the full moon, hearing stories about South Africa, myths, history... by the way, I simply loved South African music. From the playlist Andre had, I guess at least 100 songs, I was able to save the name and download it.

During the full moon in South Africa, the game rangers that live in Mozambique try to cross the board and they come to Kruger Park to take out the horns of the rhinos, to sell them, and they simply die after that. It's becoming worse and worse. Since rhinos can't see well, specially at night, when the full moon comes, it's easy to catch them. Now they are almost extinct. It's very sad, and something needs to be done to stop it.

Another interesting fact I learned with Andre and his friends is that you can't ever leave the fire on, you have to wait until it burns out completely. Not only because of the danger, it's also a ritual. Well, let me describe some of the drinks we had during that first night: gin & tonic, whiskey, Jaegermeister, passion fruit liquor, wine (white and red).

Wow. Not bad for a first day. Afrikaans music, incredible friends, braai, food and more food, drinks and more drinks and just relaxing and feeling the energy of being in the wilderness.

After a break and saying goodbye to our friends, we went back to our tent, and? More drinks, of course. The most incredible and unique moment of this night was to hear the lions roaring. We were sitting at a table outside, laughing, talking when we heard one or two lions roaring very loudly. Chills all over my body. And they were definitely not that far from us. But just to hear that sound, wow, it blew my mind.

To finish this perfect night, maybe one of the best of all the amazing ones we had, I heard what Andre and Elbie had to say about my work as an actress. Andre said: "Laura, I know that one day you'll be a huge actress, you are so talented and you put so much effort and passion into what you are doing. But please, when you win the Oscar, walking on the red carpet, do not forget about us." Elbie said: "Laura, when I read the script, even with all the changes, now, seeing you close I am certain that this character fits so well for you. Truly." (Deep breath). It's amazing to hear that from experienced people from the industry and people who truly believe in you, people who want to push you further but at the same time, are so nice and take such good care of you. I can't speak for all Afrikaans, of course. But all the people I've met during the trip were so friendly, open hearted and they welcome you with so much love and care.

We had an epic moment of endless laughing. I was in the tent, talking on the phone with a friend while Rovena, Andre and Elbie were downstairs drinking, and out of the blue I started hearing rocks being thrown on my window. I was like: "What is this?" I panicked for a second. Then I went downstairs, and no one was there. "Come on guys, I know you are hiding somewhere" I said, until I heard Rovena laughing and they all came back. They were hiding behind the car and laughing nonstop. Like three little kids. Seeing my friend Rovena laughing that way was the best gift.

After struggles and painful moments with her last relationship, there she was, shining again and alive.

For the entire week we explored the wilderness of Kruger National Park. It was definitely one of the best times of my life. Seeing all those animals free, not in cages or zoos, and being part of their world was a true blessing. We spent almost four days in the car, exploring the wildlife. Tourists and people from Africa go there to try to see the big five: rhino, elephants, leopards, lions and buffalo. We were lucky enough to see all of them, not only once but four or five times. We were also very lucky to see cheetahs. It's a rare animal to see, as they are usually hidden and because they are one of the fastest animals on earth, it's hard to see them close, yet we saw two of them, crossing in front of our cars. Moments that change your life completely.

I was dying to see lions from close. We saw some in the first two days, but only through binoculars. On the third day we went on a safari in an open vehicle. It was going to be our last day searching for the animals. In the last 40 minutes we came upon five, yes, five lions, lying together close to the river, just a few meters away from us. It was a mom and four young ones. The lioness would lick them and touch her face to theirs, protecting them. The opportunity to see their behavior from so close was a dream come true. The tourist guides recommended us not to make any move inside an open car, because if they see a different movement or behavior they might attack you. Otherwise, they just see the car as one unit, and not a car with eight people in.

Rovena and I changed places twice, to take pictures closer to the lions. Not a good idea, even if we moved with caution and slowly. When we moved, I was the one next to the lion. He looked me in the eyes, got up and stared at me. Their eyes are like fire. For a few seconds, I had never felt so scared and so much adrenaline, right there, looking into his eyes and him looking back at me. After that, the tourist guide started the car and we left.

Elbie explained to me that you can't show fear to them, you have to be brave, even if you are very afraid inside. She has one of the most incredible stories. Years ago, she was also at Kruger Park with Andre in their car, the window was open and she looked to the left and saw a big, brave, fearless lion right next to her, ready to attack. Instead of freaking out, she focused, took a deep breath and looked bravely into his eyes, showing him that she wasn't scared of him. Thankfully it worked, because after a few seconds, the lion simply left.

Another interesting fact that I've learned is that when it's time to give birth, the lioness leaves her pride and has her cubs in dense cover. They remain hidden for one or two months before they come back to the rest of the pride. The lionesses stay within the pride all their lives, but the male lions leave or are driven off by the pride males when they are two or three years old. Also, it's the lioness that normally hunts and provides food for the family. The male lions usually play no role when it comes to provide food.

During this incredible journey we also saw hyenas, impalas, zebras, crocodiles, baboons, more giraffes, and plenty of birds. It was one shock after another, so many surprises and hearts beating so fast. The best part was having two South Africans as our guides, so we really talked a lot about South Africa, the issues, the corruption but also about the wildlife and the animals. I played the photographer for these few days. Andre gave me his Canon 7D camera to take the pictures and the results were really nice.

After those days in Kruger Park, we headed to Blyde River Canyon in Mpumalanga. One of the largest canyons on earth, it also has some of the deepest, most precipitous cliffs of any canyon on the planet. We stayed there for two nights at the Forever Resort, the Three Rondavels. The energy at that place was unique and so powerful. I am so grateful to have seen so much during those days, surrounded by nature and an incredible energy and feeling, staring at those breath-taking views.

After those two nights at the Canyon, we drove

back to Johannesburg. October 8th, 2017 was the day I finally met our director, Darrell James Roodt. I was so glad to be there, meet the crew, meet my director, and everyone who would be part of this beautiful journey for the movie. Working with Darrell is an honor. He is one of the best directors in South Africa and he has worked with Patrick Swayze, Whoopi Goldberg and many other incredible actors. My dear friend Reine Swart worked with him in *Siembamba*, and she was the one that recommended me to Andre.

I felt at home in South Africa. I felt closer to them, knowing them in person and feeling so peaceful and excited at the same time. As I said before, I do believe that everything happens the way it should be. The night before we went to Cape Town, Andre served us some of the best whiskeys in the world. Laphroaig, for example, considered the most richly-flavoured scotch whisky in the world. True. It was amazing, we were sitting in the music room in their house, listening to Elvis and talking and drinking until very late that night and our flight was super early the next day to Cape Town. I was able to see when I was about to pass my limit, but Rovi - as Andre calls her - didn't, she was out and happy. But let's talk about the next day: Rovi was so, so hungover, or actually, she was still drunk. Andre drove us to the airport and during the entire flight she couldn't say a word. When we left the plane she said the most epic and funny phrase of the entire trip: "I guess am still in airplane mode". She truly was, for the entire first day at the Mother City, as they call it. Or as I would say, the Magic City, with so many wonderful sights, beaches, and landmarks, like Table Mountain and Cape Point. Table Mountain is considered one of the seven wonders of nature. Rovena and I stayed on the top for hours, just feeling that beautiful energy and taking in the view.

We found the best cafe in Cape Town, R Caffee on Long Street. It serves the best breakfast, lunch, burgers and coffee. We liked it so much that for the five days we were there, we went every single day there to have breakfast. The only time we changed restaurant was our last day, when we went to Mama Africa, an incredible place which served incredible African food.

It was a unique and incredible two weeks in South Africa. A healing, fun, adventurous trip. And unforgettable, thanks to my dearest friend/producer Andre Frauenstein and his wife Elbie. And now, the biggest step is coming up. *The Furnace*. The movie, the shooting in the wild bush in spring 2018. The door that will open for other opportunities and a dream come true. We as actors have the greatest gift to inspire, connect to other people, to put ourselves in other people's shoes and tell a story. We have the chance to explore feelings, compassion and in a way, touch peoples heart. People that might not know you, but they can link with a scene, a tiny moment on that big screen or at the theatre watching a play. That is the true blessing of being an actor. Understanding people, understanding the mess we can be, understanding all types of feelings and connect to them. Doesn't matter what role you have in a movie or a play, everything you do will make you grow as an actor, everything is an opportunity, and those moments will build into a career. You might fail a lot of times, but do not quit, never, ever. If you love what you do, acting, or any other profession, don't think about the final goal, or being famous, but think about the journey itself, doing what you love and make that the best adventure you can. Have fun with it. Enjoy every moment, every lesson. Take it all in.

Postscript

This book is about a simple, ordinary life. As I said in the beginning I am not a famous actress, I am just a big dreamer and love my craft and the journey is what really matters. I am passionate about art, life, nature, traveling, new cultures, new people, books, plays, movies... I am a person who like many others, took their chances, took the rest in search of their objectives. I had some financial stability to be able to travel and live abroad (I know I am lucky for that, not everybody has this opportunity, so I took it) and had the courage to go, leave my loved ones behind, keeping them always with me in my heart while I went in search of my dreams. All I want to do is to share those moments in this book with you, the same as I do when I am on stage or shooting a scene – I am sharing stories, we are all sharing. Around a table at a bar with friends, on a movie, on a play, or as I am doing here, telling the story of my simple life, hoping that you can connect your heart somehow – if you got to the end – to some parts of it, had some laughs here and there, kept something that might help you on your path.

I hope that you enjoyed this journey with me and found it entertaining (a little bit at least). I'll write another book when I'm 50, or 70, or 80. Maybe I will have more funny, crazy stories to tell. Who knows, maybe if you like this one, I will write another about how the journey of The Furnace continued, shooting for a month in the wilderness of South Africa, twelve hours a day surrounded by wild animals. It's going to be beautiful and tough and my heart beats faster just to imagine how it's going to be, because, one more time, that little traveler from the first pictures in the book is still here, waiting anxiously to get on the plane, just 20 years older, but full of dreams and waiting for the next adventure.

Thank you, reader out there, whoever you are. Thanks for spending a few hours with me.

And last but not least, I wanted to share what happiness means for me.

Happiness for me is sharing little moments with

the people we love. Happiness is making someone smile, happiness is helping someone, reaching out a hand to those who need it and knowing that, no matter how small the gesture was, you have done something good for someone. Because our world needs that so much. Happiness is also seeing my nephews and my goddaughter play and see those pure, naive, beautiful smiles that come from their souls. It's the sound of Quim and Tom's laughter. It's a tight hug from my sister. Even though she's not a huge fan of hugs, I hug her every day I see her.

Happiness is words and gestures of affection for my parents. Happiness is seeing my father get shy and awkward when I say how much I love him and seeing his response in his eyes and in his smile. It's sharing this Christmas day with my family, this big, silly, wonderful family. It's singing *Holly Night* together, and exchanging gifts, hugs and kisses. It's sharing the achievements and celebrate them together. It's giving your shoulder to those who need it.

Happiness is seeing a friend whom I haven't seen for so long and feel the same love, as if time had not passed. It's hearing a "thank you" or "good morning" from a stranger, or from your loved one, "I love you".

Happiness is realizing that your effort, your determination and sweat were worth it, slowly, that you are building your path and growing. It's getting a real compliment when you're down or sad. It's learning that life is made of challenges, obstacles, difficulties and being thankful for those, because they made you stronger, more capable, and taught you to value what matters most in life.

Happiness is to grow older. It's seeing the years go by and being grateful for the lessons, the experiences, but not letting those harsh lessons take away the innocent and dreamy child inside of you.

Happiness is also not losing hope of a better place, having faith, being thankful for being alive and wanting to be a better person every day.

Happiness is in the simplicity, in moments. It's sitting at a bar table, having a cold beer and remembering the good old times with our friends. It's studying, learning and rising after a fall and to get up and follow with even more determination.

Happiness is also learning to accept the 'no's' in life and to say no as well. It's receiving a surprise, it's traveling, exploring the world. It's LOVE, to fall in love, to feel loved and to value that moment. They say "it was not meant to be". But I believe that everything in life was meant to be, yes, in that instant, was right, and may not be more. But for some reason it happened that way. It's to meet someone and to feel as if he/she was your best friend, an energy that cannot be explained.

Happiness is believing in something that warms your soul before you go to bed. I am thankful for my quarter of a century, these 26 years with their joys and sorrows, ups and downs, for the learning that I have lived and for managing not to give up on my dreams, no matter how difficult they have seemed sometimes. I am grateful for the greatest love in the world, my friends and my family. I am grateful to be able to work with what I love and still be this dreamy child inside that has so much to learn and is so happy and excited for what's to come.

———⟞◯⟝———

A friend of mine, Sarah Blondin, was a big inspiration to write this book. Her podcast Live Awake has touched the deepest parts of my soul and heart, making me believe in my own self and that we are all in the path we should be, but that we have to take a look within ourselves and be in real connection with our inner being for truth and guidance, not outside, and be thankful for every single part of this journey called life. So here it goes, in her encouraging and beautiful words:

The storm has come to wash us clean. You'll find yourself and your heart again if you choose to turn toward yourself. To land on your seat. With your heart open. Simply ARRIVE and stop the running, watch each of your choices be still and calm. Choose again - one step forward, one choice. One after another after another. Not one wrong. Not one that is not in service to you. Close your eyes now and lovingly arrive at your own feet. Let your worries, your sorrows, your heartaches, your dread, your shame, your loving spread out before you... Let be a blanket of warmth and love and symmetry. Nothing you have chosen is wrong. Nothing that you have chosen does not fit into the fabric of your life. Be still now, here at your own mercy. You are in the process of writing a concerto. Of divine compassion and love. You are learning in all of your choosing. You are remembering what you are. Please, hear me when I say, there are no stains on the quilt of your life. If you choose one next thing, choose to arrive here like you have now, to give love to each part of you grown distant from your center. This is the earth that will create movement, and momentum in direction of your heart. Arriving here often will help you to choose more of what will bring you joy. Will help you LOVE your journey. Breathe in and breathe out. Be washed clean of your worry. It's time to remember, dear one, you are born to feel all of this. Let go for one moment longer, waist no more of your time worrying something has gone wrong, for in retrospect, my love, you'll see through a clear glass the pieces that came together to make your heart beat wider then it could the breath before. It's time to remember, dear one, that life is in your favor. That YOU are in your favor.